D0853286

ALL MY SINS
ARE RELATIVES

*The choice is between the
chance of tricksters and the
drone of cultural pride
on the reservations.*
Gerald Vizenor,
Dead Voices

ALL MY SINS ARE

RELATIVES

W. S. PENN

University of Nebraska Press

Lincoln & London

1995

Library of Congress
Cataloging-in-Publication Data
Penn, W. S., 1949–
All my sins are relatives / W. S. Penn.
p.   cm.
Includes bibliographical references
ISBN 0-8032-3709-X (alkaline paper)
1. Penn, W. S., 1949– . 2. Nez Percé
Indians – Biography. 3. Nez Percé
Indians – Social conditions. I. Title.
E99.N5P467 1995
973'.04974–dc20 94-36937
CIP

For Grandfather, who knows;
For Rachel and Willy, so they may.
For Pat, Anne, and my family who made
the way;
For Jennifer who helps me go;
And for Dad, after all.

CONTENTS

ILLUSTRATIONS

following page 132

William Penn (father), ca. 1934

Nez Perce women and men on
ponies, Idaho, 1870s

Nez Perce women and men displaying blankets and quilts, 1890s

Osage Agency Building, Indian
Territory, 1890s

Albert Penn (great uncle), Howard
Spencer, Joe Shakahmore, Osage,
Oklahoma, 1910s

Osage Trading Post, Pawhuska,
Oklahoma, 1910s

Adopted Osage baby on cradle board,
Pawhuska, Oklahoma, 1910s

William Penn (grandfather) in casual
dress, Anne, W. S. Penn, Clara Penn,
and Patricia, ca. 1955

William Penn (father), ca. 1940

Robert Penn (uncle) in uniform,
ca. 1940

ALL MY SINS ARE RELATIVES

THIS CLOSE, COYOTE

I

Some people say "KI-yote," it's true, but to us his name has always been "Ki-YO-tee." As our song says, "Coyote, coyote, nothing but coyote."

This also is true, and it is said this way:

I was thirteen when the barber laid bare my high forehead, waxing a roll of hair to roll like a Dreamer's curl across my widow's peak. Only the curl felt good. The rest felt naked, bare, exposed to rain, and the elemental cruelty of chewed gum stuck in my hair by boys who instinctively picked on anyone who was different. And I was different. But at thirteen, I had no idea how. I didn't look that much different. I was not as different as the black kids who looked and dressed the part. My friends were Mexicans or thugs, neither of which ever achieved sufficient numbers at school to be securely a minority from which I might be excluded. Once I had battled the aphasic thugs to the ground, sat on their chests, and made them try in their wavering white voices to chant one of my songs, we were as good of friends as I ever had – which means we said "Hi" to each other, hung out behind the gym at lunch where we smoked and told old jokes, and left each other alone. And alone I liked to be: I came from a culture that was neither transported nor downtrodden; it had been truly removed and all but destroyed but now was mostly just plain ignored outside of Saturday afternoon movies, and what I saw in the movies made me ashamed.

Father was ashamed, too, and a measure of his solitude was that I didn't know he was. Whenever the subject came up – and it did come up, what with Grandfather living nearby and with Father's brother enshrining pictures of Young Joseph, the Nez Perce Chief, all over his bungalow — Father looked away, into the distance, across the playground or football field. I never felt as though I could ask, "Dad, why do I feel so alone?" or, after a week of school with my friends, "Dad, why would I rather be alone?" It was a split: on the one hand, feeling an aloneness akin to loneliness I'd try to join, dancing the Mexican Hat Dance eagerly in cultural studies or playing games like basketball with an uncanny, almost innate ability to target the hoop with the ball. And yet after the dance was over and all of us stood around grinning, some sheepishly, having enjoyed ourselves together, or after the hoop game ended and the boys pounded me on the back with congratulation, I felt, well, uncomfortable. I smiled. They wanted me to be one of them. And though just minutes ago I had wanted to be one of them, I found little joy in being one with them, especially because I knew — somewhere way behind my eyes and underneath the words I gave them — that I could not be like them.

This wasn't the way blacks describe the feeling of being the only black in a room of whites. It came out of race, perhaps, but it was not racial. It was why, when finches flew across the street, I called out greetings to them, "Good morning, Juncos! How are you being?" It was why of all animals, my favorite was the frog, and why to this day I wear a scarab-frog necklace around my neck. It was why Father looked away from the mention of Indian things, perhaps. It was not a feeling that came from being different on the outside, the way blacks become different on the inside because of the way people treat the outside. There was that, I suppose, but it was later, secondary to my inside feeling that not only was I different but I was uncomfortable not being different. I could succeed, be a part of the Great Society around me, just like black kids were beginning to do; but where the black kids, the Chicano kids, the transformed, rehabilitated thugs and thuggettes seemed happy to be a successful part, it depressed the hell out of me. Somewhere inside of myself I knew that the measure of success was not false – not necessarily – but that it was not mine.

Thus it is that Indians fail. It is not that they cannot do it. It is because they reach a point beyond which they cannot summon the heart to travel. I've seen Indian college students read and understand Heidegger, Binswanger, Sartre, and Ortega y Gasset as easily as they understand the movements of junco or salmon and yet fail to attend the course's final examination – and for that failure, they do not get A's for recognizing the true relation of philosophy to examinations. Choosing to return to their homes before the school term was officially over, leaving college to take care of itself, they fail the course. I've seen the same students return to college the following year, only to bother not to turn in the final English essay because their brother called them home. I've heard professors say that if they can't cut it, then they should receive failing marks. I've heard other professors say they just need counseling, help integrating into the college environment, role models of Indian professors and then they will be successful. And I've heard a full range of sayings in between, even from my father's, my sister's, and yes, my own, mouth – and they are all wrong. If you are a Pit River, a Modoc, an Osage, Flathead, or a Nez Perce – especially a Nez Perce, who knows with his heart – and you are enrolled in a class – English, philosophy, wildlife management – and your heart calls you home, you are right to go.

I've seen my father, denying his Indianness with every fi-

ber and vein, come This Close to success. In the world of
money and work, he spent seventeen years getting up early
and driving downtown on the Santa Ana Freeway, an Indian
man riding a Spanish general to a Saxon building where he
plugged his knees into a desk like all the other desks, smiling
when one of his friends stuck gum in his hair, looking forward to the weekend when he could mow lawn or mend
fence and on Sunday take us to see his father and mother.
My mother, who liked the week, felt indifferent to Saturdays, and hated Sundays, was glad when Grandfather and
Grandmother decided to pack up their objects and move
four hundred miles to live next door to my uncle. I sometimes wonder whether she'd have so gladly bought new slip
covers and curtains if she'd realized that, within a year, Father would have our objects packed and move us all north-
ward to be close to his parents. We would have lived next
door, probably, except Mother put her foot down, and we
skidded to a halt some seventy miles short, close enough to
resume Sunday visits without having to live, as Mother so el-
oquently put it, in a hellhole like Napa.

Mother was embittered by the notion that in less than
three years, with just a little more gum in his hair, Father
would have had full retirement from the company he had la-
bored for all those years. She thought she could see that his
heart had called Father home, and she was bitter towards
Grandmother. Grandmother, not Grandfather, was the one
who said day-to-day things, who gave things quick and immediate shape in unstoried words, so perhaps Mother had
reason. But the blame was too great, swelling like the bitterness in Mother's heart, until she could accuse Grandmother
of wanting Father to fail. "That was why she had them move
north in the first place," Mother would say. "She was evil,"

she'd say later, after Grandmother was cut like a carnation from the earth. "Less than three years. Can you imagine?" she was still likely to ask, even after she and Father had been divorced by bitterness. "A witch."

Perhaps Mother was right. Perhaps Father's heart had called him home. But as Nu-mi-pu, as a nontreaty Nez Perce, it was in his blood to carry Home with him wherever he went – or, more precisely, wherever he was forced to go. There was something else at work, some power Mother did not see, could not see – indeed, which I never saw until it had worked in me, and even then I didn't see it, I only heard it, felt it in my heart while I made up excuses to satisfy Them. It was the power to be true. It meant that for seventeen years, Father had smiled when they put gum in his hair. He had come to believe in the value of gum, in what he contributed to society by helping an oil company extract and refine and add lead to fossil fuels or develop new chemicals which would rid the world of pests, and he could rattle off a list of things that would not have been but for this contribution. When he quit, he did not quit because he'd changed his mind. These things matter to him forty years later just as much as they mattered to him then, and I've seen him envelop his wife's head in a spraycloud of pesticides to free her from the nagging buzz of a housefly; proof that he does not believe in "all this non-sense about carcinogens." The only change in him is that he has great difficulty smiling, and he has, over the years, quit just about every group he ever joined. So what made him give up full retirement, give up all the smiling he had done?

It was not changing his mind. Nor was it the heart calling him home, as powerful as that might have been. I know this. I know that after three years of graduate school at the University of California at Davis, after smiling my way right up to doctoral examinations, after believing completely and wholly in the importance of the seventeenth and twentieth centuries, after reading white, black, Hispanic, and Indian writers who were alive all around me until I could chew gum with the angriest gay black man in the Confucius Bar at New York's MLA, after being able to quote, proudly, whatever the seriousness of the occasion, "I have my J&B. The J&B company keeps manufacturing it, case after case, year in and year out, and there is, I am told, no immediate danger of a dearth," making Donald Barthelme's *Sadness* into a kind of deflective shield, after filling out every possible triplicated form in the world, one summery day I packed up my old Volkswagen with my objects and drove eight hundred miles north to Port Townsend Washington. I never thought of it as quitting or dropping out. Indeed, years later, I discovered you needed to ask their approval to leave and that, the way General Howard had pursued the Nez Perce and destroyed their provisions, they made it impossible for me to return peacefully and take up where I had left off; they were too angry over the fact that I had just left in the first place, as though my sudden leaving were a judgment of their value and proof of my character. I certainly did not think of it as failing. I thought of it as a success. "There was no one fit to examine me," is what I said to people who asked why. But that was only an excuse they could understand, both in its meaning and its sheer Coyote arrogance. What I meant was, I came This Close to success by another measure and realized – as it appeared in a dream – my own measure was all that mattered to me. And it mattered in a way that meant something other than criticism of their measure. Let them have their measures. I knew deep down inside that, given the chance, they'd shoot Snowbird from the sky or blow up summery frogs in a celebration of Independence. At least a part of their measure meant death. How much of the dream were you willing to give up to death in order to succeed. I'd have liked to succeed – more, perhaps, than my father throughout those seventeen-plus years – enough to cut my hair crew cut, keeping only the waxed Dreamer's curl in front. But even at thirteen, I could not let the curl go completely, although I could keep the dream fairly hidden or disguised.

II

It was my girlfriend who said repeatedly, "You'll finish your degree" with the same authority someone else might say, "You'll no longer walk the earth one day." She was a white girl, a kind and generous and loving normal person to whom I'd whispered, giving shape in words to what was in my heart, "I don't know I can do it." It never entered her head that I wasn't capable of doing it, and it clearly never dawned on her that the inability was not intellectual but emotional, almost physical. My saying that I didn't know I could do it was an inadequate and unfair way to try to tell her that it was not my head but my heart that might keep me from doing it, that my heart which knew the world held secret a dream – unsaid, undefined, unending – in which I could measure myself by their stick only so far. After three years my heart was telling me that I had just about reached the end. If I got my degree before that end was reached, it would be fine; but the coup-stick end of these ways and days was no longer a mirage out there, it had shape and dimension in here. I could see it in the same way Chief Joseph saw it, fearing it, knowing it was coming, and yet, recognizing that the path which has been traveled until you can see its end cannot suddenly be altered and made into a different path, secretly rejoicing in its coming if that was what was to be. Joseph did everything he could while not signing away the land by yet another treaty to make peace for his band. Even camped at the top of White Bird Canyon, he had a white flag flown on a pole outside his lodge, a sign to the volunteers edging up the canyon that he desired peace. But in his heart, tired of the ways his people had been measured and the measures changed, he knew that when the volunteers fired on the scouts observing their movements, he would, if not rejoice, feel relief. He would be true to the path's end which would no longer be unclear and wavering like the shadow of Snowbird or the afterimage of Coyote who is gone but as sharp as war.

Graduate school was not life or death, and to use Joseph to explain me, thereby comparing myself to him, was – as I learned in school to say – "literally absurd." To explain this to my girlfriend in these terms would have drawn from her the same confusion it later drew from editors: "Wha . . . huh?" So when she told me that I would finish, and rolled over, cupping my genitals with her buttocks and resting her cheek on my biceps, I could only give her a whisper. "I hope you're right."

With all my heart, I hoped she was right, as much if not more than Father hoped Mother was right if she ever said to him, "Don't worry, you'll make retirement." It's an If but not so big an If. Probably, given the vituperation Mother expressed about Father's having given up full retirement because of that evil woman my grandmother, Mother said it as many times as my girlfriend said it. Nothing else would account for the vehemence of her vituperation but long expectation suddenly disappointed. After the first several times telling Father not to worry and receiving no reply, or none more expressive than "I hope you're right," Mother must have thought the matter settled. Or, when Father said "I hope you're right," perhaps Mother replied, "Is that a threat? What do you mean by that, you *hope* I'm right?"

I opt to re-remember the former, even though Mother was a white woman whose sense of family was perverted by suspicion and greed and whose sense of marriage was skewed by a family dedicated to divorce. I forget the latter because it is possible Father thinks he has said what he has to say. Riding that Mexican general's freeway downtown to the Saxon building, the Indian man dreams, doubling back over the same territory, making sense of it, describing it, saying what has to be said until he expects the person to whom he has said it all to understand what is true. Chief Joseph riding to a meeting with General Howard holds the meeting with the general before he even arrives, and the understanding is so good and perfect that the meeting seems almost unnecessary – and Joseph takes his time and arrives three days late. What do three days matter when the understanding has already been achieved? It is such a perfect understanding that Joseph believes that General Howard has had the same dream, has spoken and heard the same words, and their meeting is only a formality, a show for the people who do not understand – the journalists and reporters, the squatters, prospectors, thieves, the army wives who write letters to St. Louis about savages hanging about laughing at Christmas carols during this wretched season at Fort Lapwai.

When the eighteenth annual Christmas Party rolled around, Father mentioned to Mother that he was thinking about not going. "You have to go," Mother replied.

"But. . . ," Father said.

"No buts about it," Mother said. "If you don't, they'll think you don't like and respect them."

That was sufficient to end the conversation: not wanting people to think he didn't like them when he did was a powerful argument for going. A Nez Perce can respect his worst enemy, as long as that enemy is true and not conniving or hypocritical, ever as much as Joseph respected Howard, whose heart he knew, but not Sheridan, whose heart was convenient. Father had spent the energy of seventeen years saying to himself that his enemies at work were not convenient but true. He respected them. He liked many.

This time Mother rides the Santa Ana Freeway with Father. It is a happy drive because all the words Father has needed to say to Mother to explain what was going on inside of him have already been said. There is no tension. To complete the vision, only Mother's presence where the words have been said and resaid was necessary, and there she is, beside him in the finned Plymouth, all dressed up in muted colors and simple jewelry with, finally, someplace to go. Father is so content that he takes no notice of the discordant notes in Mother's orchestrated anger when he refuses to pay a valet to park the car and they have to walk a long block from the covered garage beyond the building. Her lips are pursed. He sees that. But he smiles. "What warrior pays a boy to park his horse?" he thinks, assuming Mother's lips will unpurse at the thought and her mouth grin with his. He leads her in to the Christmas party.

The party is held in the central reception room, a large open area off which spin the corridors of offices. The hall from the elevator is like a Huron gauntlet, men and women raising their champagne glasses threateningly and calling out Father's name instead of inflicting blows with clubs or feet. The light is bright like the winter sun, reflecting off the cold crust of the walls. By the time Father and Mother pass the third group of glass raisers, Father flinches; at the fifth group, his head ducks involuntarily; Mother casts him a worried angry look. At the colon of the hall, where the corridor opens onto the bright and decorated main room, Mother squeezes in smiling as Father stops. To her, it is a room of gaiety and noise, of smells and sounds of people having fun together. To him, it is a web and tangle of different stories – of so many different stories that each one seems a lie. Each is true in its way, but said in a crowd like this, words gets lost, tangled into other stories, rise quiet to the heat of ceiling lights and fall like lies to the floor, unheard.

Afraid of trampling on their stories, Father physically cannot enter that room. His best friends are there. He sees one talking to the president, and he makes a start for the corner they're standing in. Stops. A woman he cares little for nods and smiles at him tentatively; she is willing to let bygones be gone, he can tell, and he takes a step or two in her direction and then falters and returns to the edge of the corridor. He bites his lip. Then he grins and stands there, grinning until he can no longer hold the grin, and he lets his face relax into an open inexpressive look, a look that says neither "Look at all this fun" nor "I need to go potty." Just a look that says, "Wha . . . huh."

When on the drive home Mother says, bitterly, "Well that was fun," and Father says, "I'm glad," he means it every bit as much as when he says, just before pulling into our driveway to bed down the Plymouth for the night, "I hope you're right." In between "That was fun" and "You'll make retirement" there was a whole conversation in which Father explained why he might not finish out the year in the Saxon building, how finishing twenty years no longer seemed to matter. Poor Mother never heard these explanations.

Their perfection would have been spoiled, anyway, the way it was when, Berkeley a dissonant chord of lights behind us as my girlfriend and I drove into the rich darkness of the hills, I tried explaining how I'd rather be shot through the teeth with a Henry rifle than sell Death Insurance for a living.

"It's life insurance," she replied, her head turned away, her voice bouncing off the passenger window of her car while I drove.

"It insures I'll live?"

"No."

"It insures I'll live longer?"

"No."

"It insures someone will get a lot of money if I die."

"Yes."

"Best not to tell them about it, hey?"

"I hate you sometimes."

"I pay someone money so when I die they give a lot of it to someone else. So what it insures is my death, not my life. If it was life insurance it'd pay me to stay alive. Imagine. Every birthday some guy in three pieces comes by and . . ."

"I'm gonna kill you."

"I should warn you. I'm uninsured."

"It was my Christmas party!" she exclaimed.

"I don't believe in Christmas."

"I work with them. I have to see them every day. They were nice to you. They all tried to make you feel welcome. No, but all you could do was stand in the corner and sneer."

"It was a grin."

"It was a sneer."

Grin. But once I'd passed a mirror at a party and happened to catch my face grinning, and ever since I understood how to some people the grin and gruff of Coyote looked like snarl and sneer. "All right," I said. "I'm sorry."

"Huh," she said, willing to forgive me right now but wanting to say some things she felt obliged to say. Nez Perce, I was finding out, were not the only ones given to having conversations in their dreams. Women do it too. "If you were really sorry, you'd change."

"You're right," I said, wondering how people changed more than their words without dying first. Coyote, the arrogant buffoon, dies, tricked by his own trickster nature; fox steps over him five times saying words only fox may know, and he is reborn. "I'm sorry."

"You'll try?"

"What?"

"To change?"

"If that's what you want," I said dully. There was warning in my voice, threat, change. Frog preparing to bury himself beneath the mud of a Sonoran Season, dead to the world as July and August peeled the desert to its vibrant core. But how?

"I don't think I can do it," I said as we left an Oakland A's game. It had felt good and queer to sit in the private box of her father's company beside third base. Good, for the privilege. Queer, because I did not belong among the Day Care and Mutual Funds of the other privileged in the box. One man kept talking Fidelity to me, a topic I coped with by nodding until it dawned on him that I had no idea what he was talking about. "I'm talking money," he said. "Ah," I said, glancing at his wife. "I see."

"You can do it. You are not a failure," my girlfriend said.

"No, indeedy," I said.

"Good," she said.

It was this goodness that made me say to her, that loving and generous and kind normal person, when she asked if I didn't want to come over to her house and at least talk about my decision to leave school and town and her that night, "No." The words had all been said too many times.

I felt bad as I drove north with sinking heart into the mud-dark night. All the time and energy she had put into me would be a waste for her. If I were lucky, though, she'd think me the failure.

III

This is better than true: By the time I was fifteen, my hair had grown back to a respectable length. In between, I found God, the Christian God, the one whose magic is to divide himself into three forms and pounce upon the world when it isn't looking. The Front Man they use to steal your land. The one they believe has a Reason for the horrid awful thing that has just happened to them and who keeps the happy things a mystery. He must have been a real trickster to watch the volunteers route Looking Glass under the white flag of truce, not long after so many of the Nez Perce had willingly taken up Christianity and its Book. Its magic seemed so powerful.

God explained why I was different. And he forgave me. Every Sunday, I rose early and walked across town where I sat outside the church and watched the old people park their cars by sonar, backing into one car, then reversing forward into another, turning the steering wheel this way and that until, within five feet of the curb, they were satisfied. God forgave me for enjoying the vaudevillian antics of the near-dead.

He also forgave me – sternly, I might add, with a black-and-white suit of words from the minister who caught me – for nipping a couple of cookies from the kitchens on my way to Sunday school. And he taught me, after the first time, to rearrange the cookies to look as though none were missing, a skill that has given me knowledge in return. I know if someone has gone through my medicine cabinet or my drawers; I know what someone's medicine cabinet contains even though not a single label is turned or changed on the bottles and vials. I can be in your house and not disturb your dust.

Most of all, he forgave me Cindy. She was two years older than I was with a round, open, freckled face. She believed just the right amount. She spoke in tongues, but she did not throw herself on the floor and writhe like a savage. Cindy sang in the choir, and when I heard her singing and surprised her in the bushes, across the stream from church, God was there. He looked away at the local Sparrow when her blouse fell open and a breast dropped into my hand; He blinked, slowly like a window shade drawing down, as her pleated skirt drew up. Afterwards, she knelt in prayer, and I believed from the fervor of her voice that God forgave her. Me, well, maybe there was a little doubt in His mind about me. Try as I may, these cookies were a bit more difficult to rearrange. I fell asleep to the song of crickets while Cindy prayed and dreamed of mallard duck girls giggling after copulation.

The real magic of Cindy's God was that he let me be so sure he existed in triplicate that I could walk into a room of strangers and smile, certain that I was superior to anyone who saw in me anything other than a Christian. I belonged to the Youth Group. We played basketball against other Youth Groups and won. We staged wholesome musicals for the church community. We went on retreats where I got to teach Cindy how to feel the animals watching us while she prayed excitedly. We planned a mission for the summer, taking our

Triceratops God down to the Navaho (with Hopi Land) Reservation in Arizona and, while doing Good Works, preaching people into silence, if not acceptance and conversion.

At Second Mesa, the bus parked below the village perched like Peregrines or Red Tails along the rim of the mesa. The broad road, hot and white with July, the gravel sharp and glittering, the dust thin and pervasive. We followed a path until we were among the village kids who were as happy to see us as a truckload of Mars Bars. Cindy handed me her camera, posed herself, hugging two of the kids, and said "Chee . . . eee . . . eee. . . ." Her smile, almost natural at first, turned hard with effort. "Sah," she said. "Gee whiz," she scolded me. "Take the picture."

The kids were happy to be hugged all over again. They giggled. An old woman stopped in a doorway and watched.

"Chee . . . eee . . . e . . . ee . . . eee. Sah."

I held the camera. It sweated in my hand as I drew a bead on Cindy and the two kids. But I could not pull the trigger.

"Gee whillikers. You're hopeless," Cindy said with as much anger as her Christian heart could muster. "Give the camera to Steven. Steven will you take my picture?"

I relinquished the camera to Steven, who snapped off a couple of rounds, and then handed the camera over to Cindy.

"You're a real failure as a photographer," Cindy joked as we walked through the village to the quonset hut the girls were to paint a donated green. "An utter and complete, useless failure."

I joined the boys, digging trenches and holes, laying sewer pipe and planting a septic tank.

That night, Cindy wanted to be shed of me. I left her in the vestibule of the mission church and hiked back out towards Second Mesa. I turned back silently when I ran into Indians guarding their fields below the mesa walls and met Steven coming in from a roll beneath the Pleiades with Cindy.

"Hi," Steven said nervously, sniffing snot made to run by the clear night air. "There's KI-yotes out there," he added, as if to explain his nervousness.

I grinned.

"Where you headed?"

"Bed."

He was relieved.

But before dawn he was shaking me awake in my sleeping bag. "Cindy's sick," he hissed.

"Wha'd you expect?"

"Wha . . . ? Huh?" Steven said.

The following day, Cindy felt pale and hot and rested on the air-conditioned bus as we took pick and shovel and continued scarring the earth for sewer trenches. Steven worked close to me, almost severing my toe with the point of his spade. Sweat dripped into the folds of my eyes, and periodically I had to pause with the pick and catch my breath, wiping the sting and looking out at the hot fluid haze of the desert. A hawk floated on currents of air drafting up the side of the mesa. Saguaro Cactus threw their arms up at the white sky. Somewhere in the canyon, frogs were buried three feet below the earth's surface, waiting patiently for the Rains to invite them to the surface to join the celebration.

The old woman appeared in her doorway, again, watching us. Watching me. As I turned back to my pick, raising it with the joy of one who belongs, on a mission, doing Good Works, a feeling much like fear, like the anxiety of night falling dreams, riffled through my veins. I looked at Steven, at the way his stubby penis swayed in the stretch cloth of his cutoff sweatpants, his knees you wouldn't wish on a camel. I looked at the other boys, secure in their sunblock and boots, secure in the goodness of their work. I remembered Steven, in the middle of a close basketball game at the Youth Group hall, twisting with epilepsy; as people rushed to his side, I stood apart and watched. I saw the pictures of opening night and my eyes, my musical eyes that shone like crystals among the other eyes of the chorus, and remembered how I – the lead – was supposed to walk out in front of the curtain and in all seriousness sing, "Phoebe! What are you doing?" Except for the afternoon wedding of Cary Costello, my sister's friend, and the gay man with the champagne tray, I might have succeeded. I could not be sure whether I got so drunk because I was scared or because I felt This Close to success at doing something Father or Grandfather never would have done, put themselves before a boast of audience, an audience joyful and willing to accept anything I did as the authentic actions of people like me. And I reheard Cindy, as she and I sought a private arbor, crashing through the undergrowth on the retreats, intent on our arrival and not the journey. That was why Steven's stubby penis was so pointed, today, in his sweatpants.

As I raised my pick to strike again, I saw the old woman through the sting of sweat, watching, watching, and I dropped my pick. I walked to her in her doorway.

"Wha-huh," she said. "The boy who walks alone."

She motioned me indoors.

Her name was Laura P. (She warned me never to reveal what the P. stood for.) I made her my grandmother in a book, and although she never was, in most ways she is. The inside of her home was dark, and the mantle was a shrine with candles, red-white-and-blue bunting draped in symmetrical half moons on either side of a triptych of photographs of John F. Kennedy. The kitchen at the back was brightened by an unshuttered window, and I sat on a bar stool as she fed me fried donuts and piki, a fragile bluecorn roll of flake the size of a tortilla. The sweet toasty lingering taste of piki comes to my mouth even now, and I have often wished I kept the things she told me more in my mind.

The truth is, I knew what this woman said, have known it, and will always know it, without tense or time, in my heart. I ate piki with her that day and the next, and then our grim Christian bus began its roundabout way back to where we came from. In my suitcase I had packed ten rolls of piki she gave me, and a small clay bowl, thrown and etched with sticks and glazed with signs. In my heart I carried a hidden joy, wanting to remain behind and yet longing to be at home.

Cindy rode the bus more ill than ever beside Steven Shovel-Toes, and that evening in Jerome when I offered to go off with her and she ceremoniously and weakly told me no, her words rose up the presbytery to meet the undusted words of her elders, tangled in them, and fell to the floor at my feet. My heart was full still with the words of Laura P. as Cindy explained it all to death. I bit my lip, grinned, and then unable to hold the grin any longer, let my face relax into inexpression. I felt neither bitterness nor jealousy but only an odd and historied contentment that the path had reached its measure. A touch of sorrow that Cindy never would be healed. But what could I do? I had offered.

"Wha-huh," I said, leaving the church, passing the Grouped Youth playing Frisbee in the twilight, and climbing the Cleopatra mine.

By the mine was a ghost town. By now, probably, the ghosts

have been driven out, their stories ironed smooth, and the town restored. Then, the feeling of being alone was sufficient for my joy as I climbed weather-grayed steps and dusk dark stones, weaving around and through the brush that had overgrown the old mine, trying to avoid the air shafts which were covered by rotted wood. I felt as though I had the coal of fire in my pants pocket as I sat on the steep mountainside and watched the last tines of light rake the valleys below. A dark-sinned man carried a coil of rope on his shoulder. He walked across a plateau below me, past a rundown Catholic church and into a wooden cabin nearby. A light flashed on in one room. He moved a chair into the center of the room, and then the curtains closed on the window. A priest emerged from the side of the church cassocked and hatted – one of those wide French-brimmed hats – his old body shaped like the hiss of an *S*, his head hung meditatively in sorrow or understanding. He, too, crossed the plateau and after knocking, entered the same cabin. Time unwound itself. I was still sitting there hunched over my knees like Ollokot (Frog) when I realized it was blanket dark, with the lights of the Pleiades and the reflection of the moon giving everything a crisp shadowy feel like the first dusting of snow gives a white fringe to the trees and rivers. My skin felt cold, but with a jacket coldness, and the chill didn't penetrate my dreaming bones. The light in the cabin was out; the church nearby was empty and dark, its batted belfry like a finger jutting up against the starlit canvas of the valley behind it.

It was quiet, as though I sat buried beneath the earth, except for the crickets chirruping away and the occasional hoot of an owl. Abruptly everything went dead, quiet. The crickets held their breath, and the wide-eyed owls fell silent. I froze, breathing slowly, stilly, the air shallow in my lungs, just

enough to keep from gasping. Brush crackled. A stone tumbled loose and bounced all the way to the plateau below. Still
I sat, and stiller. I felt no fear, only the expectation which, in
the heart, is knowledge. To my right, an animal snuffled. A
low growl.

And then a leap, and I saw him. He stood on a boulder not
ten feet from me, still snuffling and growling, silvered with
the dust of night light, his eyes burnished with reflection. He
stared at me. I stared at him. He was this close. I didn't speak,
at first, and then it all came back to me with a rush like water
over Beaver's dam, and I felt flooded with words.

"Wha-huh," I laughed. "Ki-YO-tee. Ki-YO-tee."

2

DREAMING

Peace is meditation, not a compromise with power.
Gerald Vizenor, *Dead Voices*

I

It frightened what life was left out of the people who successfully, in the courts of an artless new nation, defended
their claims to land not their own. But even worse than the
fear was not being able to understand why the Nu mi-pu
would practice what appeared to be a religion which was
contrary to their own good. At first, things had gone so well.
Hard on the heels of the Original Indian-Givers, Lewis and
Clark, who left sick and accepted back healthy horses, they
sent missionaries to help the Human Beings discover the two
ends of life, hell and heaven. At first, the Nez Perce had been
willing, even eager, to believe in the god who had made those
two places; his power seemed great, and the Nu-mi-pu were
not stubborn with stupidity – they were willing to modify
their beliefs if it meant a better journey to the afterworld.
But now they seemed to be turning away from what the missionaries told them to believe. They seemed to be turning
away from everything, no matter how often it was explained
to them that it was for Their Own Good. Hard to imagine,
but even the code of laws developed by the Reverend Henry
H. Spalding and Dr. Elijah White, a missionary doctor dis-
missed from his last post because of his extensive lack of
qualifications, seemed to become objectionable to these Human Beings. Did they not see that being hanged or whipped
for any offense would protect them from larger retributions
from the settlers? Did they not have recourse by means of

appeal to the unctuous hand-wringing precursor to the U.S. Congress, Elijah White?

White recognized that the Nez Perce raised horses. Fine. But their herds were so vast, at times, that something had to be done to protect the farmers who plowed up the land. What was objectionable to a law which simply said if anyone "enter a field, and injure the crops, or throw down the fence, so that cattle and horses go in and do damage, he shall pay all damages, and receive twenty-five lashes for every offense" (McWhorter 1992, 65)? Why would these Nez Perce who beyond a wild Victory garden of berries and camas roots did not believe in plowing the earth, these Nu-mi-pu who had ranged over this land freely for hundreds and perhaps thousands of years before the missionaries came to donate the laws and regulations to a proper life – why would they break down a fence and why oh why would they object to anyone who did publicly receiving twenty-five lashes?

It's a question.

. . .

The worst thing a Nez Perce may say about another man is that he is a "bad man." Henry Spalding and Elijah White and the missionaries who emulated them were. As primitives, the Indians seemed to think whipping was humiliating, and in one of those strange connections of Dreamer minds, the laws and punishments invented by Dr. White and the (not so) Reverend Spalding suggested that the one true god of these missionaries might be one who was not so true. Somehow these laws the missionaries enforced (it was for their own good) began to seem to the Indians made-up. While some of them overlapped the inborn sense of justice through which Nez Perce live and had lived long before the coming of Lewis and Clark, these new laws began always to seem convenient only for the fencers and plowers and not the Nez Perce. Chief Tipyahlahnah Siskan (Eagle Robe) was shot for telling Larry Ott to stop fencing in his garden land. James Reuben (who expended his life being a "good" Indian) makes up a list of all the Nez Perce killed when he is trying to get some of the imprisoned Nez Perce freed, and that list sits "somewhere" in Washington DC. Another Nez Perce leads miners to a gold vein and is murdered thereafter; a Nez Perce is hired to help loggers, and once their task is finished, he is killed to avoid paying him his wages. In no case do the Elijah White laws punish the killers. No one goes as far to arrest a murderer as across the unpaved street where he is bragging about it in the saloon. They are only Indians. Not enough of them left to worry about anyway.

And, as history tells us, these are just exceptional instances. The truth is, let a Nez Perce break down a fence or challenge a settler's right to take more of his land, he must be whipped. For his own good. No doubt it hurt the parent more than the child. When Mother used to lay into the bared thighs of my sister with the back of a metal hairbrush or when Father backhanded me and sent me tumbling across the living room, it was for *our* own good. And it always hurt Mother more.

The Nez Perce Creator provided for a bad man to be punished in the Hereafter, journeying through an empty wasteland, a *lonely* wasteland, until he has made up for the bad he has done and finds his horse, who takes him to his people and friends. If he is an especially bad man, it takes him a long long thirsty journey just to find his horse, let alone spot the smoky distant signals of his friends or family. The mission's god provided two places, a "heaven" in which everything was just dandy and a "hell" in which their god provided a magical fire which burned bad men forever. The only good thing you could say about the mission god's "hell" was that, given the way the missionaries and their followers behaved, getting sent to "hell" was so difficult as to be nearly impossible.

The Catholic or Black Robe god, true enough, provided a third Hereafter in which some bad men could make up for the bad they had done and eventually make the journey to heaven. These Catholics were a lot like the Nez Perce Dreamers, even in their kneeling. It made Catholics uncomfortable when the primitives, kneeling to perform their own ceremonies, looked so much like Catholics. When they sought the Bishop's advice, it was poetic in its simplicity: "Make them stand."

So when the Methodist laws began to seem convenient and their god made up and the Catholics began to seem embarrassed by their resemblance to Human Beings, it was almost funny. When a Nez Perce warrior was whipped or humiliated, he had to find a way to live *through* the humiliation. He needed a way to make the humiliation not count because it was administered by bad men who did not count, and it was then that the volunteer seeds of another way of looking, another way of acting upon what he knew in his heart to be true, germinated and sprouted. The Nez Perce turned away from the beliefs and practices, the lifeways he had tried to adopt; he turned away again, back toward the practices he had tried to give up without success. Each man and woman, in slightly different but essentially identical ways, relearned the power to turn away.

The practice of turning away was called dreaming. For their turning away from Protestantism, the Protestants would desecrate Peliyivi, the basaltic column into which a Nez Perce had once been turned like Lot's Wife, removing the column to the site of the Spalding Mission site, named after that seriously bad man, and bolting on an unplayful plaque identifying it as a memorial. For turning away, these Dreamers would be chased all over the West, pursued between fences and fields, most of the way to Canada; for turning away, when they were captured, they would have their Dreamer's curl over their foreheads shorn.

There was nothing a Dreamer could do about it because from the time before Lewis and Clark his fathers had known it was to be. It frightened the settlers so much, perhaps, because a Dreamer is honest. No one likes the company of a more honest, unfrightened, prouder man, especially if his own existence is predicated on dishonesty.

Not long after it had frightened what little life was left out of people with sick hearts, they decided to find it funny.

"They dream things in or out of existence," these people said, mostly by writing. "They believe that if they dream you off of their land you will go. Hah hah."

Not quite true.

. . .

Grandfather dreamed me into the world. "I knew you were coming," he said, once. I was small, if such a word could ever be used for me, probably about eleven years. I hadn't asked, but the question had been nagging at me from the time I understood what Father meant when he said I was not supposed to live. "You gave new life to your grandfather," he had told me over and over, long before I could hope to understand, but making me wonder about the old life my sisters must have given him. "And then . . . well, the doctors said you would die. I asked if it would be painful and they said no, that you would just sort of go to sleep. I was glad."

Father tended to stare into his hands like an open book

when he told me this, what he meant by these words complicated by denial. He did not mean that Grandfather was
heartbroken over the news. It was that Father – for whatever
reasons – did not dream anymore like Grandfather. True,
he attended a Holy Roller church where people knelt and
rocked, and he had the instincts of a Dreamer who cares
about such things as peace and a proper end to the path of
life, no matter how short one's path on this earth might be.
He liked to be out of doors. Yet still Father spent a good deal
of his life dodging the temptation to dream, an effort which
turned him not away but towards, turned him into an au-
todidact and expert on English, and made him into a man
whose order and cleanliness (and Dreamers are exceptionally
clean and proud)[1] transcends the personal and becomes a
judgment on others.

The judgment is severe: twenty-five years ago, I visited Father who, hearing I hadn't changed the oil in my car since it
was discovered on Indian land in Oklahoma, took me out
and handed me a drain plug wrench and made me change it.
It was done under the pretense of "Well, let's do it," but since
my objections and promises to do it later went unregistered,
it was only pretense: I did not have a choice. It was to be.

Doing things with Dad – as much as I hate to say it because
he is old now and deserves not to have to hear these things –
frightened me then as much as dreaming frightened white
settlers. His resistance to dreaming – his, in the language he
had made his own, success – made him as tense as a rattler.
And yet you could not escape the dreaming that was going
on despite his resistance. Once, when I was leaving for
school, he kept telling me to watch out, which I did – watching out on the left as I backed my car into his car on the right;
he'd known it was to be, and all his warnings only made it impossible for me not to dent his car.

So changing the oil was doomed. I was doomed. But I had no choice. Dad had already made it be. I knew in my heart that what was to be was bad. I tried to pay attention and nervously drained the dirty oil into a pan he lent me. I was careful not to spill a drop. I removed the oil filter – in that car it was an aluminum double screen – and cleaned and rinsed and dried it. Things were going great! I replaced the oil filter.

"Tighten the nuts just enough," Dad warned. "Too much, you'll strip 'em."

I tightened them just enough.

"Here's some oil. I buy it over at Thrifty Acres by the case. Guess I can spare four quarts. Hah hah."

I thanked him. I carefully removed the filler cap, set it top down on the driveway, gently slid the self-tapping spout onto the first can and even more carefully tipped it into the filler tube. Not a drop dripped. I smiled. In fact, I beamed. Dad sort of grinned. It was all but over, now; maybe the dream in my heart was wrong. I fell for the hope: three more quarts after this one. What could happen? I stood up. I happened to look down. I saw a trickle of oil running towards my foot, growing wide like the Yellowstone River as it descended the driveway. I looked down in horror. I looked up in hope. Dad was not beaming.

"Shit," I said, making things worse because in his success Dad had decided swearing was bad. Didn't matter. I was knee deep in shit and I knew it. "God-damn-it," I cried, figuring to deflect his attention from the oil at my feet. I tried to slide under the car and put in the drain plug on the oil pan. Somehow I'd forgotten to replace it and Dad's Thrifty Acre oil was passing through my car like the flu, going in the top only to come right out the bottom.

Things have changed, since then, but not entirely. Twenty-five years later, Dad looks down at the driveway which he has just had resurfaced again and says, "I remember the first time I had this driveway done."

With most fathers, that adolescent error would've become cause for hail fellow humor but not with mine, so I don't laugh and say, "Me, too." I hold my breath for a second, having had years enough to know what was in my heart, then and now. I always had suspected myself of having left the drain plug out by fated design. Dad would not understand that in my heart I was glad that I'd forgotten to replace it, then, because he had made it be, and now, because it meant that the dream – his and mine – was real. Mine remains a dream in which I do not want to be his pal in daily activity; I want now what I wanted then – to be his son and have him notice how unimportant oil and roses were. It had been only a small dent in his car and it was only a car. His having grown up poor, though, the son of an Indian trained three years as a welder at Haskell Indian Institute, made me understand how my thinking "only" could hurt my father's feelings. So, understanding something of what was in Father because in different measure it's in me, I diverted his attention to his beloved roses – purple, red, yellow, pink, and mixblood. Over the years they have scarred him, his hands and arms, much more than any son could possibly do and yet he has always cared for them as though their thick woody branches were little more than tender pale green shoots.

II

Dreaming is not unlike the habit of walking out of rooms while people are talking. It is as though somewhere in your heart-mind you have already heard what the person is saying and entered that other room, and yet the timing of it, the variance between having heard it and having the other person finish talking before your inertial movement carries you out of the one room and into the other, is often bad. It resembles what people call "absentmindedness" and yet there is no absence. Rather, when my wife says, "Don't just walk out of the room!", there is a presence, a joining of my life of waning words and feelings to the great journey of words and feelings and actions that was Grandfather's and Grandfather's mother's. I turn away from anger – or overheated love – and turn toward something which to most people is not, evidently, real. And yet it is real to me; it allows me to survive. I already know what is going to be said; I know even more certainly what is going to happen; fight against it, I may, but I see it – having already come and gone in my heart – coming. It is like hearing the first chord of a song and not only recognizing the song from that one chord but hearing the finished song – as it was finished last time or the time before as well as how it will be finished – because it must be – this time. It is an instant and complete and whole recognition.

It is dreaming, but not of a kind that may be explained by rapid eye movements, and thus I never mess with my dreams, day or night, in rooms or out. For me – as for Grandfather – the psychoanalytical interpretation of dreams is a way to define and capture an important way of knowing, pigeonhole it so that one can avoid the instantaneous knowings, the sudden revelations of truth and sometimes responsibility. Psychoanalysis, to a dreamer, is a superstitious practice which takes the story and sting out of dreaming and puts in meaning in such a way that the encapsulated "meaning" inhibits revelation of past or present and the recognition of the future come into being. In my experience, which perhaps is not wide enough, people who tell you their dreams and then tell you what they mean are anthropologistically trying to avoid what they may mean. I am always a little embarrassed when people tell me their dreams, as though they are telling me private things which I wish they would keep to themselves. Grandfather never told me his; they just were and when they were you could tell by his face that he'd known they would be.

When I hear a dream-tale coming, prancing stolidly like one of those Spanish show horses, I usually say, as quickly and arrogantly as possible, "Dreams are boring," hoping that people will get the hint enough not to make me watch those overbroken horses, to keep from giving away these little pieces of themselves, forcing me to accept the burden of the knowledge in them. But I suppose that's as unreasonable as saying that filamental love attaches itself to the imperfections, not the perfections, and hoping that then people will not lift their skirts or drop their shorts to show off one of those "imperfections" since the minute you say "Dreams are boring," your auditor is compelled to prove you wrong by telling you one he or she thinks is interesting beyond belief.

Perhaps it's night dreams – those rapid eye movements – which are boring and private and not the daylight meditations of a Dreamer? For night dreams (or so we've been told) are vivid and fragmented correctives to the imbalance of rational daytime activity and pretense; if that is true, it seems as though there should be an awful lot of white night-dreaming going on well into the false light of morning and even unto noon. Daylight meditations lead to balance – or something closer to balance – an understanding of what is not important enough to keep you in the room if your inertial movement has fated you to leave it. For someone who believes in the wavelike action of dreaming, there is less need for those vivid nighttime correctives, and on mornings I wake up having had a colorful night dream I may say to my wife that I had strange dreams, but instead of offering them up for analysis, I say to myself that it means that I must practice some daytime meditation to push the cause of those night dreams back into the perspective of understanding. Night dreams usually mean that a Dreamer has stayed in some room too long. He has lost his balance of understanding, which cannot be corrected by night dreaming or its "interpretations" but only by daylight meditation or the activity of dreaming – which means walking out of the room because it also often means that he or she has been sucked into the world as invented by someone else's story.

. . .

Anne Marie, my eldest sister, is the biggest Dreamer of the family. Over the years, she has, through a combination of pop psychology and innate common sense, refined her dreaming almost to seeming inhumane, and she is able to turn away from humiliation or unjust pain even before it is inflicted. Signs of her Dreamer heart and mind have always been apparent. By now, she is a storer-up for the long snows she knows must come, and as an urban mixblood, what she stores up is money – not dollars, exactly, but backup resources which insulate her from the whims of fate and fortune; she is *Better Homes and Gardens* neat, everything with its place and everything in its place, the brass rails on the stairs polished and not to be touched by even a toddling two-year-old's hands, making people with children uncomfortable to stay in her house; things she does not want to do – like cook someone a birthday dinner – she not only does not do, but the idea that she might or should is dreamed away until the birthday person is having fun cooking her own dinner, and if Anne wants to eat half the cake the night before the party dinner, she'll do that, too, without a hitch. She is a gatherer and gardener, not a plower, and the hours she spends outside in sweats and garden gloves resemble Father's, except she does not sing or hum while she gardens, and the variety of flowers and shrubs and flowering vines is much greater than Father's roses; she re-members herself by dreaming almost every day – discarding every tidbit of the past – and by that means, she has found a way to live through the huge pains and small humiliations she has been made to endure, like an anthropology professor at San Francisco State making her stand before the class so others could file by and observe what an epicanthic fold looked like. If you cannot accept these things about Anne when you fly two thousand miles to visit her, you will be unhappy; unhappiness does not exist for her, so even were you to tell her, she would not believe you. If you invite her to visit you, she'll say, "Oh, I never fly anywhere that isn't for fun" and not mean it the way it sounds but only that flying seems so unnatural to her.

Anne, I suppose, began to refine her dreaming around the time Grandfather told me he knew I was coming. But it was this most painful and humiliating experience of her life – a miscarriage and the discovery that for physical reasons she'd best not try to have children even if they were planned and the way people then treated her, with relief as well as with a kind of condescension – that began her long journey toward almost absolute dreaming. Midway along this journey, twenty-five years ago, she fled from my father's and stepmother's house in tears – the occasion that had brought us together and turned unhappy was my nineteenth birthday dinner. A Dreamer may turn away and leave, but she never flees like that, so by then she was only skilled at turning away publicly; she had not mastered the dreaming art of turning away on a personal level, and therefore she still had much distance to go. Further than my other sister who'd fled my father's house in tears on my eighteenth birthday; not as far as I, who fled the same house on my twentieth birthday, frightening my then still living mother so much with my anger and humiliation, which she saw only as hysteria, that she called my sister, Pat, and had her get out of bed and drive down the Bay Shore sixty miles to ask me what was wrong.

Years later, however, Anne has surpassed us all and her ability to turn away always surprises me. It's a measure of her ability that this past summer, when my two sisters visited Father in his house and at dinner – a dinner liberal with drink if my stepmother or my father's children have anything to do with it – my stepmother turned the conversation to raising children and in my absence said that my sisters had failed my father where I had succeeded because they had not "given him" grandchildren.[2] Anne – who had replaced the potential for children with three and sometimes four dogs, for whom she cooked and cleaned – said quietly, "Excuse me," wiped her face with her napkin and folded it neatly, slid her straight back chair away from the leafy table for six and said to her husband, "I have to go to the bathroom." She went as calmly as anyone goes to the bathroom. Having perfected the dreaming art, she turned away at the instant of pain.

Probably – the conversation having turned toward children, the brother who would protest that no one "gives" a grandparent grandchildren being in absentia, the tension of my father's dinner table having built up toward the pitch that is near madness, the talk of tongues loose and slippery from drink – she envisioned the comment long before it took

on the teeth of words and started turning away minutes before the pain struck, before the humiliation of accusation
and protest, recrimination and defense could occur. My other
sister, waiting at table just long enough to be sure she was not
fleeing from it, excused herself and went to the bathroom to
find the other washing her hands and calmly fiddling with
her contact lenses, not as if nothing had happened but as if
the nothing never existed.

III

Sometimes a Dreamer may be sucked in for long periods of
time. Consider Chief Joseph, off hunting at the time the
three young warriors killed a white man in revenge for his
shooting down one of their unarmed fathers in cold blood
and started the Nez Perce War. Joseph knew in his heart that
General Howard – the man who said get yourselves to the
reservation and give up your fathers's land or I will shoot you
down – wanted a pretext for war to justify the ignobility of
his following orders and then reacting like a baby boy when
the Chiefs questioned those orders. Howard tried to talk
them into the reservation. Howard was not eloquent enough
to convince them to give up their way of life. Howard threatened, at least in part because he, himself, as an intelligent
man, felt the injustice of his position. Threats, Joseph knew
in his heart, were the words of men caught between authority and their own cowardly lack of it. Given that, when Joseph – who desired to be left alone with his band to live in
peace more than anything else – returned from hunting, he
had no choice but to join the bands who would leave their
homes rather than surrender to a coward's threats. You cannot be brave and concede to cowardice. It was an imbalance,
however, and Joseph knew it. He would rather live in flight

with his people than live with half-lies and facts, and there was no room to walk out of, only the country of the Wallowa Valley out of which the Lower Nez Perce were going to be driven anyway.

"Tell General Howard that I know his heart," Joseph's famous speech begins. People reading those words are warmed as though by fire believing that Joseph means that he and Howard are in perfect simpatico communication. But consider the possibility that in saying at the end of the War that he knew Howard's heart – even without having access to the false reports that Howard and Miles and Sturgis and virtually every other soldier and settler filed – Joseph was recognizing what he dreamed: he would have wished Howard to be trustworthy; he had wanted to believe Howard's words were, like Dreamer words, actions in their visible truth and honesty; he was willing to grant – hope beyond hope – that just one man could change from what Joseph knew he was – a military general who had to follow orders, true, but a man whose heart had chosen to join the military, whose heart must truly enjoy the taking and giving and following of orders.

Before the outbreak of hostilities, based on his past experience with representatives of Washington, Joseph knew that Howard probably would reveal his enjoyment of those orders. Faced with the frustration – and the right – of the Nez Perce Chiefs' refusing to turn tail, give up their fathers' land, leave the Wallowa Valley and be herded on to the reservation – Howard's response was the one Joseph expected but hoped against: then I'll make you. And then, typical of many men who follow bad orders, he followed that injustice with an escalated cruelty – Howard followed the order to make these recalcitrant Nez Perce move to the reservation at a time the rivers were in flood, which would put the famed Nez Perce horse herd not at risk but to death.[3] I'll make you, and just to show you I have bigger guns, now I'll make you do it at a loss.

This dream for Joseph began when he meditatively brought forth the possibility despite the possibility's being stillborn that Howard's heart knew, understood, and would modify his actions. In part, Joseph's dreaming may have proved its power in the way Howard pursued the Nez Perce as they outfoxed and outmaneuvered and outfought the armies chasing them toward Canada. In part, Joseph's dream may have failed – only a little – when he did not convince his people to keep pushing on to Canada, when he ignored Yellow Wolf's counsel and accepted Looking Glass's advice that they must rest, safely because the pursuing armies were days behind (which they weren't). They did not even back-scout the trail. Either way, Howard's heart changed as he pursued the Nez Perce, as Joseph knew it would: just as he had burst out in frustration and anger and said he'd make them move on to the reservation, as he slowly chased the fleeing people down, as he suffered harsher criticism from Washington, he slowly changed from casually wondering if what he was doing was right to having to prove to himself that do it he could.[4] The power of Joseph's dream, then, consolidated a little more every time the Nez Perce fooled the pursuing armies and every time Howard took another hit of criticism and questioning.

Some say that dream ended and another began, but I say the same dream changed, when Joseph handed over his rifle and turned his back on Howard to speak to his relatives in the oft-recited "Hear me my chiefs" or "I will fight no more forever." At that moment, as compliant as Joseph has been invented to sound, the dream changed from one in which Joseph knew Howard's heart, yet had hope and expectation that his heart would remain steadfastly good against the onslaught of nitpicking evil, to something else. At that moment, at the moment of speaking with his fathers, with people who mattered and who knew Joseph's heart, the Howard Joseph knew before the war (and who now made promises to help Joseph's people) ceased – as it had already been told would happen – to exist.[5] I doubt Joseph ever took seriously Howard's assurances that the Nez Perce would not be treated ill, and I'm sure it came as no surprise when Joseph and his people were loaded onto flatboats and removed down the Yellowstone River to Eeikish Pah,[6] the Hot Place, the Indian Territory that resembled the hell the missionaries so deliciously described where too many Nez Perce would perish of homesickness and heat and disease and where one of his daughters would marry an Osage named Penn.[7]

The dream that was and had been modified into the dream of return to join his father and his father's father, a dream which ended in a dream, a dream in which the "I" and "He" melt into another third person, a "we" who joins all the "we's" who have come before, egoless and unharried, finished with the small circle which is therefore rounded out and complete. It would be a long dream – Joseph would not abandon his people easily. Some of them would stay in the Territory. Others would be removed again to the Colville Reservation in Washington. Joseph would go with them and, even in the year of his death, he would seek approval for his band to return to the Wallowa and Bitterroot Mountains. Exiled in Colville, treated as a nuisance, humiliated and insulted, the dreaming which allowed him to go on looked to white people like one which made white people not exist. They could photograph him. They could find against him as the Indian Agent often did when he sued for just and equal treatment. In their version of his dream, they were either not there or going away. The end of their version of this dream came when Joseph turned away from them finally and, sitting for days beside his fire, dreamed his way into the happy place of his father and mother and, according to the reservation doctor who was called in to invent an explanation to go with their version of Joseph's dream, died of a broken heart. As a final irony to their version, they buried Joseph at Nespelem in the yard of a Christian church, an irony Young Joseph may well have predicted.

. . .

The people who transported Joseph's body to Nespelem to bury it in Christian ground so deep that had the spirit been still with the corpse it never would have escaped from the hole to make the journey to his fathers and his mothers, these people could not envision a Dreamer, let alone a Dreamer dreaming a dream not in which They did not exist but in which *their version of him did not exist* – as it had never existed. They couldn't envision this anymore than they could envision someone not wanting to live by their laws, to be whipped and humiliated for their own good, or to live by their religion, to be weekly whipped with words and threats – for their own good. Thus, while Joseph's dream modified into the truth as it had always been predicted by his fathers, They made up a Joseph they could live with, going forwards and backwards in their revisionism.[8]

Military and civil journalists and historians began at the identical point Joseph's dream modified, with his "I will fight no more forever" speech. They quickly erased Joseph's statement that had he known how thoroughly and cruelly the terms of surrender and peace were going to be broken he would have fought to the death rather than suffer it. Then they added and changed until it sounded as though Joseph was The Chief of all the Nez Perce, an enlarged, paternalistic authority who wanted to look for his children, rather than a man who was simply noting that his band (which to Them were his sins) were all his relatives, as in all the Nez Perce bands. Realizing, especially the following day after White Bird's band along with Yellow Wolf and some of Joseph's band, had moved on to Canada under the cover of darkness, that what they had here surrendering to them was something less than all the nontreaty Nez Perce, they covered their tracks. They made Joseph sound like the Chief of chiefs – and thus the ones who went on were criminals, sneaks who did not abide by the agreements of their "officers" – so unlike the Jacks of the U.S. Army.[9] They diverted attention from the fact by making Joseph the great tactician who managed to "elude" their pursuit. Very little was said about how inept that pursuit was, ebbing and flowing between the contradictory pulls of wanting the damned Indians just to vanish and wanting to exterminate the problem once and for all. By reinventing Joseph as a master tactician, they not only ennobled the Chief they had just conquered, thereby making their "success" all the greater, they portrayed themselves less as bullies and more as honorable fighting men, and they excused their own astounding inabilities the way all bureaucrats do.

The problem is, either Joseph was a great tactician, leading his people on a winding trail towards Canada, or he was what Merrill Beal calls him, the "camp master" (Beal 1963, 162). Besides "camp master" sounding a little like the Boy Scouts and not people fleeing for their very lives, what Beal evokes is an image much like the upper-lip Brits in World War II prisoner-of-war camps. As neat as Dreamers were known to be and as often as Joseph went through the camp urging cleanliness and neatness (Wilson 1972), it seems less than likely that the chief assigned the role of keeping camp organized would be the great tactician in counsel with Yellow Wolf, White Bird, Looking Glass, Ollokot, and others.

When they made Joseph the "tactician," they had to be careful. Too great a tactician, too great a Chief, and it would seem as if this forcing the Nez Perce to swallow a treaty they never signed was wrong. Too proud and angry a Chief, and it would make the settlers sometimes wonder if the obvious rightness of their actions and ways wasn't impossible to communicate to these savages, as if the white man and the red man were never meant to get along by means of the red man being educated into the correct paths. So besides tactician, they made Joseph a slightly unwilling participant in the flight and battles of the Nez Perce. He was away when the three young men killed some whites, and they wrote him down as a hesitant participant in the wars, rarely mentioning that Old Joseph had told his son the whites would win, hardly ever noting the seething anger – at the young men who cut off hope of a just peace, true, but a much greater anger at the way the whites had already abolished all hope of justice or peace and the subsequent determination not to live by their orders.[10]

Once you notice that Joseph was away when the War began – a war Howard and the Indian Agent very much wanted, to justify themselves – you begin to notice in the Indian accounts of the flight of the nontreaty Nez Perce that Joseph is hardly to be found when tactics are being discussed or when battles are being fought. You have to recognize that, just as Joseph's surrender surrendered a "we" that was not the Nez Perce but a "we" that was Joseph's band, so in Joseph's own accounts when he says "we" decided to take the

Lolo Trail instead of an easier route that "we" is a council. One could envision the scene with the chiefs taking counsel and Ollokot suggests that they take the Lolo Trail with the general assent of the other chiefs and then White Bird turns to Joseph and asks, "Can you get the people ready?" and Joseph replies that he can. But when the battles begin, the question "Where's Joseph?" has to keep coming up. Otherwise, Yellow Wolf, Joseph's brother (close relative) is lying in his accounts of the flight – and the humility of a Nez Perce, let alone the blood relation between the men, his firm unshaken belief in the power and justice of words, his unwillingness to lie and deceive almost to a genetic flaw, argues against the idea that Yellow Wolf would not give credit where credit was due. The idea that the military and civilian reporters would lie, well, that is not only a possibility, it has been proved time and again to be a fact.

Take this entry from M. Gidley's *With One Sky Above Us:*

Latham was the Indian Agency Physician at the time and place of Chief Joseph's death. When Joseph took leave of this life, on September 21, 1904, at Nespelem, Washington, on the Colville Reservation, it was Latham who was reported as stating that the chief had died "of a broken heart." The statement *was widely circulated at the time and soon achieved the status of an official diagnosis. It has been repeated again and again by historians . . . it has now acquired the force of myth.* (Gidley, 14, my emphasis)

Add Latham's letter to Professor Edmond S. Meany, "*I was not here at the time of Joseph's death* and regret it very much. *He was buried before I returned,* his people are all at Yakima gathering hops, upon their return they may have some doings but I do not think it will amount to much, if there is anything worth while I will try to get photoes (sic)" (Gidley, 14, my emphasis). And we begin to see the way in which Joseph is ennobled, made tragic (not that he wasn't) but tragic in a way that titillated the guilt and remorse of people who would never in a mite's life correct what they and their parents had done. Finally, add on this:

> As will become apparent, he [Latham] proved to be a representative figure of his time and place, with representative views and biases. He was not actually as sympathetic to the Nez Perce people, for instance, as his oft-quoted verdict on Chief Joseph's death might lead us to conclude. Indeed, he often thought of the Chief as a cunning schemer and of his people as overlibidinous savages. *This and others of his opinions have not been published and examined.* (Gidley 21, my emphasis)

Take one chief, reinvent him, ennoble and tragedize him even to the extent of mythologizing the doctor who diagnosed the cause of his death at a distance of a hundred miles from the corpse, name him Joseph, and you can forget about the man, himself.

It seems evident – even today – that people have trouble admiring heroes who are Human Beings.[11] Certainly it's the case with Joseph: he was a Human Being who, unlike the Methodists and Presbyterians judging him, had a sex drive; he was a human being who, in his disrespect and disregard for what Latham and others called "justice," cunningly schemed not just to make them pay to photograph him in "war regalia" (he's overdressed, if Yellow Wolf is our guide for proper battle attire) but to get the U.S. Government to allow him and his people to return to the Wallowa Valley. In some ways, we can wonder if they did not prevent his return

in order to keep his a tragic figure who wrote and spoke elo-
quently – in order, in other words, to keep him nonhuman.
We know that Lawyer and the Nez Perce who signed away
Joseph's land bitterly fought Joseph's return: the presence
of an honest, unfrightened man would create too stark a
contrast.

All this is not to say Joseph wasn't a great Chief or a great
man. And if he wasn't the tactician but only the chief of logis-
tics, he was a great speaker. Joseph knew words, he knew
rhythms and rhetoric as well as, if not better than, anyone. It
is why the dominant culture picked Joseph to make over and
reinvent, partly because it did not value eloquence and
speech and partly because in his wonderful speeches he could
appeal to white hearts, to their need to feel those twinges of
sin and guilt and remorse without redress. But it is also why
the Nez Perce think of Joseph as a great Human Being: he
used words well, he spoke truly, he swayed and persuaded
and convinced by means of the truth. Words, speaking well,
truth – all these the Nez Perce admire.

. . .

This is what Joseph knew as he sat dreaming beside his fire
waiting for his heart to stop, signaling the beginning of his
last journey. Perhaps he already saw his own mythologizing,
a complete picture of what had been imaged forth when he
spoke so well in Washington, received "heart"-felt praise and
then nothing changed. Nothing even happened. Words in
Washington were empty, only there people did not believe
that empty words were evil but the way of things, all a part of
"getting along." Joseph sat and dreamed: he turned away,
having dreamed his own invention and the consequent
death of the reality hidden in the blanket of that invention.
His heart broke not for himself – he was headed to join his

father and his mother – but for his people who would be all but forgotten in the death of the reality. For Joseph, it wasn't that his dreaming would make white people go away. It was that in his dreaming, "they" no longer existed because they no longer mattered; in the reality that had come into being as it had been foreseen by his father, one could only avoid succumbing to their inventions, and in the effort to avoid succumbing, Joseph turned away, towards his fire, and his heart stopped.

It is a lesson to all who would resist inevitability. Every history of the Nez Perce ends, essentially, with Joseph's final surrendering speech as though the Nez Perce existed only while they fought and fled. Afterwards, when they were removed first to Eeikish Pah, the Hot Place, where so many died of fever and sickness, and then to northern Washington State, far from the Wallowa Valley they loved, they existed only to be photographed and anthropologized and cataloged. Then they vanish from the face of the nation's consciousness in all but the myth of Joseph.

IV

Inevitability is tricky. Dreaming teaches not so much that what is inevitable may be altered as much as how it's inevitable.

Not many years ago, I sat on top of Tunnel Mountain in Banff, Alberta, a mountain which had been sacred to the once local Indians, a sacredness which had kept the mountain from being tunneled by the railroad, though it had not kept the Indians from vanishing in the face of the railroad's invasion. I felt calm on top of that mountain, distant and out of reach from the people who had, for the third year in a row, denied me tenure, something to which I had, for one reason or another, attached too much significance.

"Someone's out to get me," I'd said to my wife on the phone that morning. I didn't believe it anymore than she did; I knew that in a world where criticism and theory are presumed to be more important than storytelling, no one person could be out to get me – or anyone else – because there was no one person, only figures and representatives, hidden by the anonymity of false reports or closet conferences, like General Howard. Figures who took seriously their use of power, believed they were doing the right thing, and – living in an environment where people who tell the truth are hated or feared – tried very hard to be honest and fair. These figures were not individual human beings but faces on a multiheaded "They" – and every year, some of the faces rotated, new faces were glued on to the They which then went about rewarding the faces that had come unglued in an amazing merry-go-round of self-interested conflict.

To me, of course, it seemed that every time I was out of the country, "They," whatever their names, denied me tenure, raises, rewards. Sometimes I wondered if they didn't send me out of the country just so they could do it without having to look me in the face.

At dawn when I'd called, my wife had put my two-year-old daughter on the phone and I heard the voice of the little girl I call Snowbird (but who yet has to want and learn another name) ask, "Daddy, why are you in Canada?"

It was a question, and it made me begin to hear in my heart how I was here in the mountains Joseph and his band could well have reached, working on a novel to please Them, not me; how I was here, not there with my band as small as it was; how once again, things were my fault, not Theirs: I was the one who had tried to seek a compromise with power. I had taken up with the Howards and Lawyers, with the land-grabbers who, without more land to grab, grabbed up power and held it to their chests like bottles of expensive scotch to be doled out in little measure. In my attempt to make them like me, at least appreciate me, I had fallen into the same vanity of self-affirmation and self-verification that caused Looking Glass to counsel badly. Worse, caught between an authority I did not understand and my own cowardly compromise, I had even threatened to sue, aware at the time that it was only a threat, not a true promise.

I gave up writing in my hut early that day and started up the tarmac road that led to the foot of Tunnel Mountain. I was wary, my nerves on edge and my senses alert for the female Elk who had calved two days ago and who yesterday had chased me up a nearby hill as I dodged from tree to tree keeping something substantial between her feints and charges and my person. I was alert, too, to the Mountain Lion I'd also seen the day before, aware somehow that a Mountain Lion was given that name because it generally took up and then maintained possession of the one same mountain – and I was climbing hers.

The climb to the top took most of an hour. As the slope eases and the bald head of the mountain begins to round off, you have to step over fallen trees and pick your way across icy patches and strips where a slip could send you on a short breathless flight into the ice-crusted river several thousand feet below. The granite cap was marked by initials and cheerful slogans by a high school band from Toronto, an ignorant desecration that had made me angry all the days before. But today, it didn't. Rather, it made me laugh with a grim awareness of these impotent boys and girls twittering as they daubed their paints into the shape of their initials and hearts and bumper sticker slogans and how little the mountain cared. I sat smack-dab in the center of Claudette with my knees hunched up and began to rock with the light wind that swept the mountain air and gazed out over the wide valley below. Below and left were the rushing rapids of the river where I had picnicked beside the rotting carcass of an Elk and watched the force of the tumbling river carry small bits of still-red flesh away from the bones, a process that would take not only this spring but most of the summer because of the glacial coldness of the water. On a level with my knees beyond the Elk beginning its journey was the doll-sized Banff Springs Hotel where there were so many rich Japanese that the locals had developed an attitude similar to that of General Motors employees in Michigan. Friends and I had played outdoor shuffleboard on the hotel patio one night while the rich gathered inside behind huge plate glass to watch until the hotel management requested our departure. Below the patio of the hotel was the sandbar on which the same friends and I had sat and talked in slow voices punctuated by slaps at mosquitoes and the silent observing of small fish and water walkers playing out their lives.

The breeze rose towards wind and I rocked more. My heart ached with a longing and confusion tinged with humiliation.

West along the valley floor was the swamp and the farther lake beside which the friends and relatives of the Elk who had chased me were, for the most part, calving in communal privacy according to their season. The white mountain due west was all glacier inching south towards the Wallowa Valley hundreds of miles beyond the U.S.-Canada border, marked only by tollbooth shells with uniformed agents lurking inside with questions. Beyond it were the "Paint Pots," a national park protecting the place where Indians had come for thirty generations to gather the ochre clay, take it home and bake it dry, mix it with animal fat, and streak it on their faces and bodies and hides as decoration and ceremony. I had dug my fingers into the clay and coated my arms and streaked my face. My Canadian friends agreed that it was permissible for me to carry off two small lumps of the wondrous ochre without interfering with the purpose of the park. I mailed one lump to my father-in-law in the hope he'd paint me a painting out of the dye, marking the package, "Contents: Earth," and imagining their disappointment when the agents of customs tore open the package in a fury of suspicion and found not drugs or commercial contraband but a lump of ochre clay.

I rocked, the wind now less than my rocking.

The Mountain Lion showed herself to me on a ridge below and I called to her softly. She ignored me and in a leap of faith disappeared down through the trees that held the sky so close to themselves.

I rocked and began to hear voices gathering in my heart. At first it was as hard as sins to tell one from another, but slowly as I listened I began to recognize some of them. Many were old voices, some had the higher tone of newness; some were voices I had never listened to before, and some were the familiar voices of my heart – wife, daughter, sisters, grandfather, father and, way off in Eeikish Pah, the thin voice of my mother. They said that graffiti painted on stone by schoolboys who had no connections did not alter the sacredness of a mountain anymore than the death of the Indians who first found it sacred.

The voice of Joseph asked, "What's the use? You can't win with these bad men. Maybe if I surrender they'll find it in their minds to treat us better than they ever have." Then he was revised: "From where the sun now stands. . . ," he began, and before that revision was over, I heard father say, "Maybe if I act like them, they'll treat me like one of them."

I heard Henry Spalding and Elijah White tell me those were the rules and in the echo I saw that those rules were their rules invented to exclude.

I heard the unmistakable voice of my department chair say over the telephone that I'd been denied for lack of publications, and I heard my sister add – my sister who had made so many things possible – "Even though you've had more new publications in the last three months than most of the full professors in your department have had in their lives?"

I heard Gerald Vizenor, even though I did not know it would be Gerald Vizenor, say it's okay with them as long as you drone about cultural pride on reservations and don't get in their way, and I heard my sister say her weyekin was Coyote, the great trickster; mine was only Ollokot, Frog, buried beneath mud and waiting for rain.

I heard my wife who showed me love say we'd be okay. She had the courage to turn away with me, and we'd be okay. "They don't matter, so their whipping doesn't count."

And I heard the voice of my son (Bear) who was not yet born in the timbre of my daughter's voice and like thunder rising my heart lifted to the knowledge that from an early age my daughter, who had the knack of disappearing from the room even before she could crawl, already had seeds of dreaming in her way of living and I was glad that the difference would be that she will know what dreaming is. She would never laugh at it, disrespect it, try to excise it from her heart and vocabulary as I had done, taught to do it by a father wanting to be other than he was and a mother who wanted otherness just as much as he. And that evening when I telephoned with a glad heart to say I was fine and the voice of Snowbird who had taught me how to love asked her question, "Daddy, why are you in Canada?", I had the words all ready, words given to me by Yellow Wolf, words that had risen into my mind as I sang with my mouth and heart as I walked down Tunnel Mountain, sang the knowledge that a Dreamer never flees in fear and never threatens out of cowardice.

"What am I doing?"

"Uh-huh."

"You want to know what I'm doing?"

"Yes, daddy."

"Telephoning you."

"Daddy! You know what I mean."

"What?"

"What are you doing in Canada?"

Dreaming, I thought. At last I knew that they had invented Joseph to kill him; I had to invent myself, to live.

"So Daddy?" my daughter said. "What?"

"Coming home," I said.

3

UPROOTED IN EEIKISH PAH

I

Mother's weakened heart popped like a bulb of seaweed and
my telephone rang.

. . .

Mother loved *Gunsmoke* because it was a West she could
stand, a West she could have lived in because it was a West
without Indians and thus a West without my father. She
loved that one with the Cartwright Family, too (she didn't
mind Asian servants like Hop Sing who were just a little
smarter and just a little wiser than the marble-mouthed son
and his wiry brothers, Joe and Adam). At bottom, she loved
most all Western television programs and movies because at
bottom they all got rid of Indians, changed them into evil-
natured children who fornicated and stole, gambled and
drank, and who needed mother – or people like her – to re-
write their characters.

Many years later, when my father – perhaps faced with the
expectation of his own death or because of his children's activity in things Indian – finally was able to excrete the shame
he'd forced himself to swallow years ago, he began dropping
jigsaw pieces of our family's history in the post to his three
children. Packets of papers appeared like Osage runners,
one packet to Anne who threw them away, one to Pat, and
one to me, and until Pat and I began to put the bits of information together, none of it made much sense. And then by
luck I opened an archive folder at the Brooklyn Museum to
discover a picture of me taken in 1877 in Osage, Oklahoma –
a me named Albert Penn, then, but me nonetheless, and
wearing the Anglo name that in an instance of simultaneity I

had given the narrator and protagonist of my first novel: Albert, whose nickname in the novel is Alley. One of the two favorite places for Osage to go if they left Indian Territory was
the place of Alley's birth, the City of Angels that hunkers
along the ocean like a reservation for cars, the city of my and
my sisters' births. But the best news was that I am related neither to Sean Penn nor Robert Penn Warren who possessed
the indignity to let himself be photographed at eighty without his shirt in one of those mocking attempts by a photographer to make poets just like us – a bunch of horses' asses and
old stick men with sagging dugs. Indians crawled out from
behind my family tree or dropped like fruit from its branches:
Indians and Mexicans and Blacks named Albert and Jonathan and William, Mary and Mary and Consuello – "Oh,
yes," Father said, surprised, "Aunt Consuello. That's right" –
and Nettie and LaRue.

. . .

Mother once devised a kind of family tree for me, a tree lad-
dered with question marks and dead ends. At last I saw why
and remembering the way Mother had so loved her *Gunsmoke,* freed by the way she had written me out of her will
while writing in the adoptive son and asexual lover she replaced me with, I understood in my heart just how much she
and most of her family feared Indians. We had grown up
knowing we were Indian – through Mary Blue – descended
from a great Chief of a people who had many great Chiefs to
choose from. Mother couldn't deny our blood because we
had Grandfather to show us, and even she, in her odd, chill,
dry-ice way of loving, I think, loved her father-in-law. But
Grandfather was old, Father ashamed, and we were young:
she could keep us from realizing how Indian we were and
thus keep us all a little wary of being too proud of that large

part of our hearts and our heritage. She could keep us off base, ungrounded, insecure, covered up, the way she kept my little red face with perpendicular ears covered from the inquisitions of her neighbors in the housing projects or the way she put herself in the position of going to every school I attended and explaining over and over again that I was not antisocial or retarded, I was bored, put off and confused by the things they did in their schools, visits which caused her great shame and wondrous suffering over the recalcitrance of her son and yet which also gave her a kind of Anglo-Saxon pride which looks to principals and teachers an awful lot like defensiveness.

It was her nature and her upbringing to want us not to be Indian, a want reinforced by her twenty-five years of marriage to Dad, twenty of them bitter and unhappy in which her stultified frustration and loathing of his lust caused her to begin by frustrating his love and finish by frustrating him, by making him marginal, ancillary to the function of her immediate family. She even managed the discipline, sending Anne off to her closet or beating Pat mercilessly across the bared thighs with the back of a metal hairbrush, except for the beatings I frequently needed when she called him in like a dog from the yard to administer them. Then I got to feel the special flavor of Father's frustration. He worked all the harder trying to make more money to prove his worth to her, and here he had to come home to a house closed against him and a son who by making his mother angry made his mother make his father feel locked out.

. . .

In my heart, I know Mother meant well when she made up that family tree: like the good Doctor Latham who diagnosed Joseph's death from a hundred miles away, she was a product of her times, as well as of her Anglo-Saxon way of thinking, her Christian Scientist childhood, and her unimpassioned disinterest in savage activities like sex.

Proof of her way of thinking was in the way the "famous chief" Grandfather told her about is listed (with question marks fore and aft) as "? Sitting Bull ?" Sitting Bull was the only "famous chief" Mother had ever heard of, except, perhaps, Geronimo. Probably the "Sitting" part of his name helped, too, because to Mother, a sitting Indian would be a lot less likely to injure you or steal from you, and sex with a sitter — for a woman whose sexual imagination inclined no further than the unpleasantries of the position of missionaries — was out of the question. "? Sitting Bull ?," despite the pictures of Joseph on Grandfather's wall, whose people were not kind to the Nez Perce who did make it to Canada. Putting Joseph back in his place on that tree was easy enough, though, and so I thanked her for a tree which ended at the time in me.

But now with Albert Penn standing in colorful silk shirt and neckerchief and high-waisted pants, his perpendicular ears disguised (though not hidden) by his long hair, the extent of Mother's wishful thinking in compiling that tree becomes astounding. "? Sitting Bull ?" wasn't the only error: Mother took two surnames, Penn and Lee, and by using parallel lines to implant those dead ends and question marks which skipped whole generations, sometimes two, she managed to make her children related by blood to Sir William Penn of County Cork and Merrye Olde England and to the Lees of Virginia. In an open contradiction, as though to reveal the lie to anyone who would look carefully at her arborous labor of love, Mother claimed that the relation to the "Lees of Virginia" came through her side of the family. A tenuous relation, I'd say, especially since Charles "Lee" was the son of Mary Blue, who married Mary Liptrapp, whose daughter Nettie married John Penn (brother to Uncle Albert) who gave us Daniel, Consuello, Grandfather William, and Maude (who married John Hogan, Chickasaw). Our family measures how (before oil) undesirable a place Oklahoma was to the federal government that so many different bands of Indians ended up there.[1] As tenuous as was our relation to the "Penn" family, once I found Uncle Albert, I knew how to find the Penn surname which was given to my fathers and uncles by the Orthodox Quakers who were deeded the mission in Indian Territory by the federal government in its passionate interest to protect and raise the Indians it had shipped there by the hundreds and thousands.

Strange, in a knowing not much different from naming the protagonist of my novel Albert, I had never in my life claimed or admitted relation to those "Lees of Virginia." I knew they were not my people; they were rich, expected things to work in their favor and when they didn't, maintained an elegance in defeat like the gray-haired general, Robert E. Even when people with any sense of history, a generously small number, asked if I was related to William Penn, I'd say, "Yes, but not the one you think." William was, after all, my grandfather's name (and now the name of his great-grandson). All of Mother's dead ends and question marks failed in their purpose to wipe the family clean from Indian, and it has taken the years since her death and Last Testament for me to believe that it wasn't wishful thinking as much as the only way mother knew how to know. She was a sad woman and the tension between the tree and the truth would be enough to make anyone's heart burst.

II

My sisters say my parents were happy, the Indian and the Anglo, but by the time I was born, Father had been made into an unpleasant presence who was fortunately absent most of the time, except on Saturdays, when he banged on my door and invited me in his frustrated, exclamatory way outside to "help" mow the lawns and wash the car, and on Sundays when he gave us no choice but to attend the rolling unholy Baptist church with him and Mother. It was the rolling that counted to dad; the Baptist was a compromise with mom. Even on that fated Sunday when some bratty boy tore the blank leaf out of the front of my *New Testament* – a small volume that had once been Grandfather's – and I was blamed for it; even when I suspected that the Sunday school teachers really didn't want this odd little boy in their classes and especially didn't want him mucking up the stables of the Christmas Pageant to be put on by us preschoolers, which suspicion I could articulate only by asking my dad why they didn't like me; even after I was denied the privilege of being a lamb in the Christmas Pageant – as I was just being reluctantly chosen to be, all the good parts having gone to children in frocks and frills and bowed ties and not that boy in a T-shirt of broad pink and black stripes with a waist where his neck should be – because I fell into speechless expectation that the boy who did it would admit he'd done it like a Human Being; even after they found me a good distance from the church grounds, having fled from the humiliation of injustice and unfairly inflicted punishment (that other boy got to wear the name of Joseph!): Father blamed me.

"Wha'd you do wrong," he asked without a question mark.

"I ran," I said.

Dad's anger flinched, but held.

It was Mother who, detached from Father by distaste and perhaps relishing any disagreement with him, saw in me the lost, lonely, needful soul, the out-of-place soul, that she must once have seen in Father. And it was Mother whose idea of comfort was not to hold me, to let me feel the cure of speech-lessness, but to angrily denigrate what I had been denied: "You don't want to be a lamb in a silly play, anyway."

True enough, I guess. But would it have hurt me to be accepted?

Unfortunately, by the time Christmas rolled around, her anger had dissipated and she and Father made me sit in the audience and watch that sneaking little liar boy play out the feeble role of Joseph, husband of Mary and putative father of Jesus, turning my jumble of feelings onto my parents and questioning why they had made me attend.

. . .

It has taken forty years to see the red and the white of that moment of life and though I still have some questions I understand why Father said I must have done something wrong to be denied lamb-hood. This was the same man who steadfastly believed his entire life that if you did things faster, better, more economically for a company, it would reward you. Because his family had left Osage country where Indians were murdered by the hundreds for their oil leases, he had grown up unaware. He had no concept of that capitalist irony that in a trick of light and punctuation the less you do while assuming attitudes of importance, the more you are valued and rewarded. He was the son of an Indian and all he had ever wanted was for the companies he worked for to want him to work for them. He had always wanted more than I to be picked to be a lamb. But there was always that torn blank page in the Book inherited from his grandfather, that page without words or signs on which his bosses found the excuse to deny him.

The fact that he had never been picked and had at times been denied – passed over for promotion, given the shitty jobs of flying far from home for weeks at a time, excluded from parties and social groups – was not something to sit around worrying about, feeling sorry about. It meant that he just had to try harder to do a better job until at last he cracked the code and someone higher up sneaked down to tell him he'd done well. In trying harder, of course, he became twice as good, twice as smart as every other schmo in his office; he became twice as excluded because they couldn't stand someone who not only did more work than they but did it without complaint. Worse, they despised him for not taking part in the events he was invited to – business conventions where they got drunk and hired prostitutes, told lewd jokes, and generally acted out the American Dream like college fraternity boys who believe the cruder and louder they are, the more potent they are. And when he refused, they decided he was not one of the boys; they worried that he might publicize what they did; they began to hate him with disproportionate passion – and so you have this confused father, incapable of believing these things could be true except in hell. Being his father's son, he assumes that it is his fault, not theirs, that there is something he doesn't understand, some action he has not taken, some failure of his thinking and believing.

But he manages to smile, at least from the teeth, and plug away until it happens in a small tot way to his son, and his heart raises the painful question – why did it happen? – and, unable to see that it had to happen, he grows angry at the fact that his son has "it" too, and in his opinion "it" is like a disease, and so he represses his own sorrow and sadness and uprooted despair and blames the son – you must have done something to make them deny you. The question, Why did this happen? leads to the question Why does this always happen? to Why has this happened to me? – a regressive series of questions which is not infinite because there was once a time when the Nez Perce and Osage roamed freely on lands they called their own, a time when this did not happen.

It's a question that Dad has to avoid as much for his sake as for Mother's, because she's as Anglo-Saxon as they get and has been raised to smile pityingly at those who would cause her or her offspring injury, except that by means of her marriage to a man whose smile at injustice is confusion and not condescension, her pitying smile has turned to a period, an exclamation without the flair of the vertical stroke. This is her son, after all, and though it isn't quite à la mode, even she feels some maternal love for her son, so she defends his humiliated dash from the Sunday school room, the church, and the church property. But "You didn't want to be a lamb," said angrily, does not prevent the family's appropriate attendance at the church's inept celebrations of Ex-mas because Mother does not feel the humiliation. Mother was impermeable to things like the humiliation I felt; she did not even suspect the heat of the Sunday school teacher's stare on the back of my neck as we watched the colorless spectacle of that dolorous pageant.

III

Growing up, we knew we were Indian. There was, after all, Grandfather, and he told us stories no one else wanted to. But we did not know how Indian. It was a piece of laundry disguised or hidden from us: Grandfather had a brother, Daniel, who lived only thirty miles from us and we never met him. Great Aunt Maude showed up on Thanksgiving with this strange dark-skinned daughter in tow and then seemed to vanish into the unbloomed buds of the tree. We never heard about Aunt Consuello, not enough about Mary Blue, and less about Mary Lipptrap. We never heard the words "adopted out" which is the phrase that pickets the names of every single one of Grandfather's brothers and sisters – a phrase which was used only for Indian children who were "adopted" out of Indian schools by civilizing, decent white folks who would teach them how to do their work for them. We believed we were Nez Perce – because Grandfather said so, and because Mother in a too-late attempt to fathom what made Father an exclamation, tried to record what Grandfather told her, able only to record just so much because so much was not in her view of the world.

. . .

Mother allowed and Father encouraged me to participate in odd Indian groups in Los Angeles. I made my own drum, breech clout, and leggings, sewed and decorated them. I learned to dance, and performed some of them or attended others. But the strange thing was, when Father and I attended a dance, it seemed as though he was proud of the dancing while we were there but on the way home would feel it necessary to say something nasty and mean about the whole idea of dancing. If I had danced, he tried to avoid nastiness about the dancing and would just say something nasty about Indians in general – as though he was both proud and ashamed simultaneously. It was not dissimilar to Mother's seemingly instinctual and certainly necessary comments whenever I told her Indian things, comments which reminded me with that period, again, how her grandmother had shot attacking Indians from the unshuttered windows of sod houses.

It looks like a trade-off to say that while we never saw or

met great Uncle Dan – a heavy loss in my way of thinking –
we children saw very little of Mother's family outside of her
sister and four nieces whom Mother and her children visited
up north once a summer. As for her father, we saw him in-
frequently and never enjoyed it; her mother died when I was
so young that I am unable to visualize her face; and the suc-
cession of stepmothers Mother had would not interest anyone, other than to say that they were all platinum Christian
Scientists who drank and smoked as heavily as Mother's
cousins who seemed to incinerate themselves annually, one
by one dying from falling asleep drunk with a lit cigarette in
their hands.

Of course it was not a trade-off. Mother and Father never
traded anything. It was Mother's family who – except for her
sister – did not want to see us. But we did not know that then.
Who wants a bunch of wild Indian children around to remind them of the miscegenation that had wormed its way
into the fruit of the family's tree? As one of the nicer relatives
once said to me when Mother and I visited, I in my long hair
and jeans, "I doubt I would pick you up hitchhiking." Still,
she had Edna the maid see to my feed, and the next day sent
her grandniece out with me in a convertible car – Julie, I
think her name was, the daughter of a woman who'd cremated herself the year before – and while Julie was thoroughly pleasant, we stayed to the boulevards and freeways to
avoid her friends while I sat stiffly in the passenger seat
wanting with all my heart to say the right things, fun things,
and frozen by my silent tongue while my heart jabbered like
a yapping dog behind my teeth. I fell in love with Julie, that
afternoon; I fell in love with the easy way she had of being in
the world and with the way she seemed hardly to notice my
stammering silence when she asked me, her teeth like white-

washed pickets around a field of illusions, what I would like
to do or where I'd like to go or what I did or what I wanted
(which in her terminology meant "expected") to do with my
life besides live it. What I wanted to do – a vision with very
real details that had grown as one cloverleaf led to another
and we worked our way out from Long Beach – was ride with
Julie off to a life where I could learn to be comfortable and
where she could learn to be, if only for moments, silent.

When we'd seen all the freeways of Long Beach and she
returned me to Edna in my great aunt's kitchen and I asked
shyly but hopefully if she wanted to do something tomorrow,
she didn't slip and look displeased. She said, simply, "I'll
have to see."

"Thanks," I said, still blinded by her comfort. "For today."

"You are very welcome," she said. She smiled.

I wanted to say something. I wanted her to understand. I
followed her back out through the garage – past the parked
green Cadillac Uncle Ross had given Aunt Flora for her birthday – and held her car's door open for her.

"Julie [or whatever her name was]," I said, blurting her
name out to force myself to say something more.

"Yes?"

"You're wonderful!" I said.

What did I expect? For her to soften, to show the first signs
of discomfort or emotion – outside of that picketing smile
and easy banter of a one-way conversation – for her to say,
shyly, Gee whillikers, thanks, in a way that let me know that
she admired the fat, awkward, silent type?

"Thank you for saying so, cousin," she replied, and in that
way she let me know her obligation – to her aunt, not me –
and her satisfaction of it. The next day, while Mother sat on
chintz and thumbed admiringly through album after album

of her aunt's and uncle's last trip abroad, Julie called my great aunt to say that she and her boyfriend Tom had to go to the beach so she would not be able to entertain me again.

"He's a nice boy," my aunt said. "They're almost engaged. Well," she said to me, "I guess we'll have to have Edna find something for you to do."

My plans for Julie to elope with me, her second or third cousin who was only a year younger than she, seemed a little ill-founded.

For a few nights I had lustful coyote dreams about Julie until like the Chesire Cat in Lewis Carroll she grew insubstantial and only her smile remained, a smile that in its apparent comfort in the midst of wearing obligation hung heavily on the branches of my heart until it, too, disappeared.

. . .

It's funny to me now, although I imagine that it wasn't funny to poor Julie, then. There's this fat lump of umber boy in her car, and she's got to waste the day and a tankful of gasoline driving him hither and thither with the hope no one will see her – no one she knows, that is. Worse, while he's silent, which allows her to speak whatever comes to mind without really having to do much more than follow her training and upbringing, he has this flat, hangdog face and deep, heavy-lidded eyes that keep sneaking looks at her – and which she catches in the edge of her rearview mirror without letting on. She has heard about his side of the family, always with a sense of relief that it's a side well distanced from the octahedronal face of hers. Oh, well, she is doing this for her great aunt; family is family – although, ugh! that includes him, too, doesn't it?

Poor Julie. I only hope that she can laugh over that day, if she remembers it at all. For me, that day recurred often enough for it to remain in my heart until I finally learned that the cliché is true: you can take the boy away from Indian, but you can't take the Indian away from the boy. For me it was the first time I was treated like a fart in the room by people too polite and well-brought-up to even sniff as well as the first time testosterone poisoning let me fool myself into imagining that a girl like Julie would dump her boyfriend and be different, changed as utterly as I would be, away from the day-to-day influences of family.

. . .

Mother said – not often and always in my memory, unattached to specific details – that Father "made her elope," a phrase I took to be little more than her invention of an explanation of how she ended up married to Dad, and yet I remember a photo of my great uncle's about which Great Aunt Flora had calmly stated, "That was your wedding." The two pieces never fit, were kept from fitting by Mother, in a sleight of detail, expanding on the information and telling me that Dad took her out one night and would not take her home until she agreed to elope with him. This would be kind of romantic and impassioned but for the fact that after Mother's death, I found out just what night that was. Indeed, it was not the foolish young man wanting Julie to drive away with him into a world that will never exist, in which things like blood and class are erased by simple love. It was the fear of the Indian boy, knowing that he did not fit, knowing that Mother's father despised him – who and how and what he was, smart and poor and the son of an Indian – that made Dad drive Mother into the Hollywood Hills overlooking Los Angeles two days before their wedding, and make her – not by talk but by silence and stubborn immobility – agree to elope with him the next day. Elope they did. But to wealthy

Anglo-Saxons with all their breeding, one simply did not cancel a wedding to which hundreds of other purebred people were invited and for which they had all had butlers and maids and secretaries purchase and send plated presents. So while Dad and Mom were hundreds of miles away, Mother's brother and her cousin, one of the future self-incinerating women of her family, stood up at the wedding and acted out the roles of my future mother and father, said their "I do's," cut their cake, and shared it. I can only imagine the scene, and it is from having met Mother's family that I know that not one single person behaved any differently than he or she would have if the real couple had been there – except, perhaps, that there was no nagging tickle in their noses making them want to sniff. Indeed, some probably did not know it wasn't the real couple. Indeed, indeed, the people who did know that Bob and Mary Alice were not Bill and Elizabeth may well have been relieved. Certainly, the family was. Indians weren't welcome – not even Dad's dad, which may also explain Dad's desire to elope so as not to enact such a cruelty – and without the groom, no Indians crashed the party. An even greater relief was that it gave Mother's father the excuse he so wanted to hate my father for the rest of his life, without having to say he hated my father for his who, what, and why.

When Great Aunt Flora (or was it Fauna?) slipped and said, "That was your wedding," she meant it. That photo was of Bob and Mary Alice standing behind the five-tiered cake at the country club having the time of Mother and Father's life.

And a sad time it was. It wasn't just that Mother's father hated my father; it was that Mother, essentially, hated Father. It went back to the night he forced her to agree to elope with him, not to the elopement itself (though there was always that, I'd guess), but to the single flutter of fear Mother must have felt as the thought that against her father's wishes she was marrying the wrong, completely déclassé man dashed through her mind like a roach in sudden but brief light. At first she had thought this silent boy who acted so exotic and different was just awkward and in need of some training to help him into the world, but on that night she must have suspected that no amount of training would fit him to the imagined world she knew. Where he had asked questions, he was now making pleas which would change over the years to exclamations. When one is raised full of questions without many answers – Grandfather was removed and had removed himself from some of the naturally occurring answers that were around him, like his grandmother Mary Blue, that "difficult" woman – one tends to turn in later life toward questionless answers followed with marks of exclamation, and here in courtship and early marriage was a moment the punctuation began to transform.

IV

Family for a mixblood may be the biggest sucker of all. Although Father had never visited Mother's family, I did not understand why until, not long after Mother and Father divorced, drawn in by the sinful desire to get to know my English grandfather and to do something for my Mother, I volunteered to drive her the five hundred miles to visit him. I had never known him well, growing up, an ignorance that was as much his choice as it was Father's. In fact, I hadn't liked what I did know of him – he married and divorced women in chiffons, he was rich but refused to lend his daughter money when at age fifty she needed it badly, he spoke in clichés as stupid as "Seen one X, you've seen 'em all," he once sent a check to my mother to divide up for Christmas with a letter indicating that some was for each of my sisters and some was for Mother, forgetting me by purpose or on accident – which I need not have found out if his daughter my mother had simply divided the check four ways and not three and not followed his orders to leave me out and then told me about it, even showing me the letter with his very clear instructions. He made his fortune during the Depression, taking the opportunity of other peoples' suffering to prepare his profits. Other than these trivial things, I didn't know much about him and what I did know did not inspire curiosity or interest except for the fact that I carried some of his blood in my veins.

Family is family, and Mother was scared to drive all that way alone. Grandpa Hall couldn't be worse than General Howard. I was between jobs again, so I said, "Hey, I'll drive you," and off we set. Now Mother was not crazy – only a woman slightly dazed by the world would make a point of telling her son he was left out of her father's Christmas orders. Later, she would be even more dazed, inviting me to visit and when I arrived after a three-hour drive fixing and eating lunch with my sister and her husband and not inviting me and my girlfriend to fix and eat with them, pointedly leaving us out in her Anglo-Saxon exclusion, her jealous possession of the attentions and focus of my sister's husband, and her inability to have two men there at the same time. Even later, she would accuse me of saying I hated her – which my sister's husband said, but I never, aloud, and only rarely in my heart – and she would, by then, be close to correct except that I knew what hatred could do to the hater. It's a sorry thing to say but when she died I cried because I felt so wrong for feeling so little except to find my mother a bad woman; I'm still as sorry as tulips about that, but when my eldest sister tests my identification and says, "The day she died was the best day of my life," I am not horror-stricken.

I say, "I know what you mean."

But at the time I offered to drive her twelve hours to visit her father, I thought I could tolerate her company and I convinced myself that it was important to make this gesture to the buzzing, stinging side of my family. The vw I owned had a grip handle over the glovebox for the passenger to grab onto in emergencies; by time we reached Tustin California, Mother had loosened it irrevocably, tearing at its roots with every imagined emergency, sucking air in through her teeth with a wet hiss that made my heart pause. And then she talked. She talked about my father. She talked about my sisters. She said all kinds of things that I knew were no more than half-truths and by time we reached the hotel in Tustin I was having difficulty walking, let alone walking out of the room.

That night, her father spoke to her on the telephone – we were three or four blocks away, too far to go at eight o'clock, I guessed, and he'd seen his daughter three years ago. Mother and I found our own dinner. The next day was the big visit. We arrived at his house – a ranch style in a community of ranch styles isolated from contact with any but the equally rich – promptly at 9:30 as ordered, and the dream I'd had of seeing him again began to coagulate if not consolidate when I said, "Hello, Grandpa Hall."

He said nothing.

You're here for your mother's sake, I told myself. Close the door behind yourself and follow their voices – Mother's,

Grandpa's, and his Number 5 wife's, Mary's – which are receding swiftly into the living room.

Mary seems surprised that you don't stay in the entry hall. You sneak along the wall, keeping your back to it but your eyes cast down, not daring to put your dizzy feet on the oriental rug which is so ugly it had to cost a year's college tuition, and sit in a straight-backed chair with embroidered cushions. Mary's eyes grow wide. The chair creaks beneath your weight but holds. You smile. She looks away.

"So tell us, how's Anne Marie?" Grandpa says. Anne Marie, your eldest sister, is their favorite, no doubt about it.

"She's fine," Mother replies, choosing not to tell them the truth.

"And . . . ?"

"Pat?" Mother fills in. They don't like Pat as much, but as least she's a girl.

"Yes. Patricia. She's still married to that teacher fellow?"

"Bob," Mother replies.

"Good," Grandpa says.

How's that? Truthfully, old Bobber's kinda strange. He hides empty quart beer bottles in the washing machine. Nearly killed you with a glass and aluminum avalanche when you opened the closet one day. Took you out for pizza and beer one afternoon to complain about her – the first and last time any man was allowed to do that. Yep, she's real happy.

Grandpa Hall seems to have finished. He seems content. He's covered all the bases. He has had a good visit.

Well, goodbye. Nice seeing you. Thank you so much for coming. It was a pretty long drive, was it not? No problem. Only five hundred miles. We hope we'll see you again soon? Et cetera.

Mary interrupts you.

"Suzan's at Riverside, you know," says she, her tone implying that Mother does not know she has a niece, let alone one who was going to college. "She's studying French. Majoring, I think they call it. She visits us every weekend. She gets a little lonely, you see. What with young men these days being what they are."

"We bought her a little car for her birthday. Make the trip from Riverside to us easier. A little powder blue car."

"How kind," Mother says, falling into the same kind of accent these people used, an accent filled with "of courses" and "you knows" which are superfluous because of course One Knows.

They talk like this until eleven-thirty. Mother's father speaks, receives gentle correction from Mary, and Mother nods. At one point, you throw things into a panic. You stand up.

"Is there a toilet?" you inquire politely. "You needs to pee."

Even Mother looks horrified. Later, she'll explain in a hiss that in polite company one calls the toilet a bathroom. They go to the bathroom, as though just visiting it clears and cleans their unmentionables.

"Do you have a bathroom he can use?" Mother asks, trying to calm their fears. There is a washroom, Grandpa Hall tells Mother who then repeats it word for word to you, beside the entrance from the garage.

Lunch is much better. Leaving Mrs. Hall behind – she is tired or some such (she was sixty-something; she must have rested up quite a bit, 'cause she's ninety-something as I write this) – Grandpa Hall takes Mother out to his favorite restaurant, an inexpensive cafeteria just a mile away. He doesn't exactly invite you along but that chintz or splintz or whatever chair is giving you a rash in the heat, and darned if you are going to stay in it while he and Mother eat and Mary rests up for the desultory conversations of an afternoon. You stay close to Mother and hop in the backseat before he knows what has happened. He steers, pushing down and lifting up on the accelerator of the oversized car in that maddening way old people do with automatic transmissions, to make the car go, but not too fast. These people don't drive, they coast. At the cafeteria I almost get sucked in, feeling expectantly good because Grandpa – rushing on ahead with his tray – actually waits and pays. I see him take out his billfold, unfold it, and remove several bills from it and hand them over to the register clerk, who smiles.

But as you walk past her, the register clerk grabs your arm. You point toward him and she shakes her head, and in another coagulative consummating moment, having delayed too long beside the salad bar looking at all those colorful fruits and vegetables laid out like an invitation, you get to pay for your own meal. By then, you want to.

After lunch, back at Grandpa's house, you wears them folks out. You take possession of the butt-rash chair and wait. The moment their hearts – or whatever pushes the blue sludge through their veins – seems regulated, you shift in the chair making it squeal and Mary's eyes pop. You pretend you're a contestant on *To Tell the Truth,* feinting the Real Mr. X standing up. When a lull in the flat of the conversation is filled by a tour of the new landscaping in the backyard, you tiptoe up behind them and whisper complimentary words, giving him a red red rash on his white white neck. Back indoors, she repeats everything she's already asked and answered them about Pat and Anne, refilling them in on what your sisters are doing, their successes and failures, their hopes and her misperceptions of their dreams, until three-thirty or four when she and you leave to return to the hotel. He stands at the window the way his mother's mother must have done, waiting to shoot at renegades from the windows of her sod house.

Having been prepared by dreaming that all this would be, you are pleased that in an entire day with your mother's father and stepmother, sitting uncomfortably in their living room in which little living was ever done, not one person had spoken my name. It was safe. I had been there but buried like a frog in the desert mud, waiting to emerge with the spring rains. Now we knew again what it was like to have people wish you were not there. And we now knew the weakness of their wishing. We could ignore their existence because wishing was not dreaming and they were not Human Beings. Even though I'd spilled oil on Dad's driveway, the weakness of their wishing turned us away from Mother's family and aligned us completely and finally with Grandfather's family. When Mother's father took ill just before he died and Mother called, we said little. In my mind I thought a sentence that would not bear revision: Tell Grandpa Hall I know his heart. Imitating what he'd do if we had died, we went out and bought a magnum of the best champagne we could afford, chilled it, and when Mother called with the final news, drank it, hoping the while that her father believed in the Christian Hell. If not, his journey through the Hot Places will take a long, long and lonely time – long enough, I hope, for him to want to call my name as I pass him on horseback, wishing only that he could remember it.

v

It's been eighteen years since Mother died, and still I sometimes wonder if Mother has seen him, walking along stiffly, glancing over his shoulder now and then as though expecting a Cadillac limo to come to get him at any moment. Mother in the same shoes she wore five miles every day to school, stuffing newspaper into the toes to block the holes in winter, the same shoes her father would have let her wear even after he accumulated everyone else's money to his accounts.

Mother spent seven years calling me on the telephone nearly every night, developing my fortitude against a curiosity that frustrates my wife who simply must answer a ringing phone. She was going nuts, during those years, excused by my sister who thinks her brain was not getting enough oxygen. Oxygen or not, her brain sure was getting its share of hateful ideas, and every night she'd call and share them with me. Her telephone calls hunted me down in Davis California, Port Townsend Washington, and San Simeon California, and most nights I took them until she realized she hated me and she ceased to call me altogether. I had made the mistake of trying to tell her how she'd beaten Pat with a hairbrush all those merciless years, and Mother could not forgive either the truth or the person who said it. Pat forgave her and, daughter to mother, tried to share her feminism with Mother, but in the flash of Mother's synapses what was political for Pat became, not unlike radical feminism, personal for Mother. In this Brand X feminism, hating men and yet unable to do without one, she became a one-woman club, a club which favored only my brother-in-law who was a male but was also as sexless as a saint and thus unthreatening, with whom she replaced my subtraction and with whom – even though he'd said he hated her to me – she was girlishly in love. He lived in her house. When she died unexpectedly of an aneurysm and coarctation of the aortal valve – which means she went quickly and painlessly (for which mercy I am glad), holding my brother-in-law's hand and saying, "Well, this is a fine kettle of fish, we've . . . " – the "we" of the lover or wife was cut short by the burst of her heart.

We had her cremated for four hundred dollars and sat through a memorial service at which I wept from laughter until I dreamed the minister into the shocks of flowers behind him. Mary, my difficult great-grandmother, had been difficult because she'd been cut off from the place that made her in her heart. Loaded onto flatboats with the rest of Joseph's band and transported to Indian Territory, removed in the sin of progress from land and family and from the crow of Howard's "victory," unable to swallow her bitterness and hatred and anger, she developed a "sharp tongue" to keep the people she hated at bay, and in doing so kept the people she might have loved distant. It was hard reality that changed Mary, whereas with Mother it was that moment of wishful romanticization in which she imagined you could change an Indian by the beneficial contact with her people who were already willingly detached from place and for whom being detached seemed, almost, necessary to their way of life. All Mother's detached people had left to hold on to was class, and in the moment that Father's silence convinced her to elope – a moment which was like all their moments together, including the one in which she said "yes" to his proposal – Mother had detached herself even from her class. Out of her element, she developed a devious brain and a skewed tongue. Her words became both hateful and frightened. Sitting there in the pew at her memorial service, I swallowed my anger which had caused most of my pain and gained access to a solitude that would not be broken by any petty temptations to rebut people who grasped my hand and said the only words they knew to say about my mother. When one old lady said,

"She was such a generous woman," I did not answer, "She was not."

"She could be," I replied.

To a man who said, "She was one of the kindest. . . ," I said, "You knew her?" with a gentle inflection that disguised the question and made it sound to his middle-class ears like an affirmation, even though Mother was not, in the end, a kind person.

The daughters of my mother's sister filed up and hugged me and Vicki asked, "How're you doing?" and seemed to understand the way I said, "I'm doing good." Neither she nor her sisters nor I was aware that this would be the last I'd see or hear from them for fifteen or twenty years.

At the least, Mother was like so many people who begin by loving Indians and end by hating them or their children. She was jealous and small, and after the service I sat rocking in Mother's living room alone, re-membering myself. Remembering Mother cornering me when I came home with a head-dress or Elkshead-painted drum or ankle bells for dancing and telling me how *her* grandmother had shot Indians from the windows of her sod house. Remembering Mother instinctively turning to wrap her son in her arms as Father's car was broadsided in Glendale. These all fell away and I began to understand that all Mother had ever tried to tell me was that she hated men: and Indian men were to Mother, having been married to Father, quintessentially rapists. I also saw that in her way, when she made up that elaborate family tree with questions she wished had remained questions and dead ends she wanted to keep dead, she was trying to give me her heritage, to make me notice that only part of me was Indian. I understand it now because I've noticed how many Coyote stories I tell my daughter, and how often I tell her about the creation of Human Beings during the Christmas season when she hears all those stories about Baby Jesus. Fortunately, with my daughter, the Creator is probably the same Creator, and she is a Human Being despite the Jesuses and Josephs and Marys. Shooting Redskins was probably Mother's sharp way of fighting against my blood and the influence of the Indian groups I belonged to.

The words in her will, carefully and cruelly substituting for me my brother-in-law by name and heartsickened love, helped by the same lawyer who had gotten me out of jail time and again during my teenage frivolities, caused me to turn away in pain and in joy. I was sorry she left this world so bitterly – she now would have to follow the trajectory of those words across the desert on the same path as her father. Though her written words stung like a wasp, I was happy because – as I've come to realize only more as the years have passed – I knew in my heart the hope of freedom. At the moment my brother-in-law read the will and stumbled in surprise over the words aimed at me, a dream began and it was a dream of a home and family that resembled the ones before the diaspora Grandfather and I had grown up in. For our people – the descendants of Lawyer, who signed away his people's land, their valleys and sheltering mountains, as well as the descendants of Ollokot, Joseph, and Yellow Wolf who traveled far and long to avoid making a compromise with power – always were and are family people.

Mother signed away her right to be my family and with her last words tried her best to keep me from having one by freezing my anger and making it bitter like Mary Blue's. But she began to fail the moment I turned away leaving my eldest sister behind to toss Mother's ashes in the backyard of a house sold to strangers. Anne Marie, casually and with unequaled sanguinity, opened the red plastic coffin-shaped prefabricated box of Mother's ashes, shifted out the baggy closed with a twist-tie and, untwisting the tie, strewed the gray seashell chips of my mother at the foot of a honeysuckle vine. An irony as sad as Joseph's deep and Christian burial at Nespelem.

4

PITCHING TENSE

Every Sunday, Grandfather rose, showered, and dressed up in the formal attire of a former welder. Khaki shirt, khaki slacks, khaki tie hung down his sinking chest without tack or clip. His pants were pressed with a lick and a promise that would outlast several washes in the old wringer, his shirt starched and his tie so flat it looked drawn in magic marker. He poked around in his workshop where the files and saws, torches and vises rested in their quivers and clamps and, with everything in its Sunday place, he settled down into the slatted armchair on the porch and waited for us.

"It is a good day for dreaming," he might say with a wink. Not that dreaming things in and out of existence was funny – that's why he wore the tie and why his mail-order shoes mirrored the light in the ginkgo trees. But it was a happy activity, a hopeful activity – and Grandfather was given, always, to laugh. When Mother passed the serving plate, he'd wave it away, announcing, "I don't *do* broccoli." Or he'd turn suddenly on my cousin, sullen and confused by school and pie, and say, "Would you shut up? You're always shooting your trap off." Everyone but Bobby laughed.

Grandfather didn't do cheese, either, although by saying he didn't, he meant a good deal more than simply sticking a cheeseboard cracker into his mouth. He meant that he preferred not to go to some winery in the Valley where they would sample cheeses while looking askance and askew as if making a peace with their tastebuds. When Grandfather preferred not to, he took up a position of refusal – slumping into slumber.

One of these cheesy Sundays, I was in his living room, reclining on the Salvation Army sofa while Grandfather sat like an Egyptian in his armchair. In the dinette-kitchen, my father and stepmother were planning with Grandmother to go cheese and wine tasting. Again.

"Two hours, Mom," Father could be heard saying. "Do you good."

"I don't know," Grandmother said. You could hear her wiping her hands on her apron, smoothing downwards, a gesture with which she measured many of her considerations. "What about Dad?"

"We'll take him," my stepmother answered. "Be good for him to get out."

Grandfather's eyes were already closed. Immediate as the punctuation in stepmother's sentence, he fell to slumper. His head dropped back, his arms gave up their hieroglyphic stiffness, and he began to snore, turning up the volume one tick at a time so that by the time Father appeared in the living room to ask, the answer could be heard throughout the house.

Father looked at his father, and then turned on me. "We're gonna go cheese tasting," he said to me. "You wanna come?"

I yawned. "No, thanks," I said. "I've got some work to do. I'll stay and keep Granddad company."

"You sure?"

"I'm sure," I said. "Maybe take a nap."

Father nodded, returned to the dinette kitchen and after a few minutes of fussing and chatting, of putting on coats, deciding they were too heavy and changing them for button-up sweaters, coming back through the screen door with a wooden bang to grab the coat just in case, a mixture of voices directing and encouraging and trying to be patient, they left. I listened as a hunter listens, trying to identify each sound as the car started, backed out, and drove away. I breathed slowly, quietly. We were out of danger. A minute passed. Maybe two. By now, the way Father drove, he was probably out on the main road tailgating a semi. Not long ago, he'd actually tried to bump the rear fender of a car on the Bayshore Freeway because it was going too slow. Out of time in the beginning of his life, he would have time on his hands at the end; it wouldn't be very long before he flipped over the coin and stubbornly drove one mile per hour under the speed limit in the fast lane himself. For now he was in kind of a transition between tailgating and, once he was cited by a highway patrolman for following the patrol car too closely, going doggedly slower than the speed limit.

No matter how fast he went, he saved his brakes, putting them on only at the last second with sufficient pressure to not quite slow the car enough for the turn – and definitely not hard enough to bring his car to a stop before it interfered with the personal space of the car in front of us. I imagined the quiet drivers of the Napa Valley, the Sunday drivers whom Dad despised though one himself, weaving erratically, their eyes pinned like binoculars to their rearview mirrors, wondering if that glaring, gesturing man behind them was really going to ram them at twenty miles an hour. Fortunately, my grandmother had never driven a day in her life; nor had she been in an accident with Father driving. She had no idea what could happen, of the sad foil crumble and tear of Dad's car being broadsided by stubborn miscalculation. My stepmother's eyesight was bad and the cars Dad nearly rammed seemed distant blurs. Time for them was passing pleasantly enough in spite of the fact that these days time for Dad was always tense.

I reached for my book. Grandfather's right eye opened. It swept the room, discovering the spiders that were let to live, the motes of dust drifting in the light from the front window, the flowers dying on the mantel, cut and arranged by my stepmother. It stopped on me, held by the laughter on my face. The other eye opened.

"They gone?" Grandfather asked.

I nodded.

"They'll be back."

I nodded again. "Not soon," I said.

"Cheese tasting," he said.

I shrugged.

"I like cheese," he said.

"I know," I said.

Grandfather straightened up in his chair. He looked at the waiting television, a black-and-white in a mahogany cabinet with doors that could swing shut and cover the screen, making the unit look like a hutch. The doors were never closed, in part because someone might leave the TV on behind them and what would happen to the world without anyone knowing? Open, the mahogany panels served as blinders, focusing attention on the screen. I had seen Grandfather stare at the dead glass so long that he seemed almost lost in its blankness.

"Head cheese is good."

"Yeah."

"How's school?" he asked, gazing into the screen as though the answer would appear there.

"Okay."

"Jack."

"Jack, too," I said.

"What are you learning?"

"Nothing new."

"Huh," he said. "New." He pointed at the book I was reading. "What's that?"

"A book. For English. *Frankenstein*."

"Not the one smell like dead elk."

"Limburger."

"He Jewish?"

"Cheese."

"This Stein fellow."

"No," I said. "I don't know. He's a doctor. Dr. Frankenstein."

"He's Jewish, name like Frankenstein." He stared at the blank TV screen a minute. He was often missing Los Angeles. The housing projects. His neighbors were Jews and though the insides of their homes were as different as east from west, in their neatness, their bright-light resistance to decay, their polished presence and dignity, they were the same. Where the Steins had placed an upright floral vase, Grandfather had put a squatter handbuilt pot, but the feeling of family was the same, and the palpable smells of food mingled in the air behind the apartments like friends.

"What's it about?" Grandfather asked.

"This doctor creates a monster out of the parts of people. The monster learns to feel sorry for itself and goes around killing the people the doctor loves. The doctor lets the monster kill his brother and stepsister and best friend and wife and father – everyone except one brother – before he decides to do something about it."

"Sounds familiar," Grandfather said. One could not grow up with removal in his blood and mistake what Grandfather meant.

"Yeah. 'Cept this guy, Frankenstein, whines all the time. He screws around with creation and then he whines. He feels real sorry for himself. The monster, too. He whines. He says misery makes him malicious, strangles all these innocent people, and then goes on and on about how bad he felt the whole time he was doing it."

"You know these people?" Grandfather said. "I know these people."

"I go to school with 'em," I said.

"Never did me any good," Grandfather added. "Cheese did more good."

"Than school?"

"This story, why do people tell it?" he asked.

I shrugged.

"Is it real?"

I shook my head. He wasn't asking if someone actually made a monster that ran around killing his family. He meant true. Was it true like the stories he told me. "Made up," I said. It was a novel that, despite Captain Walton's dating his letters "17— ," could only have been written in the rise and flush of Romanticism.

"They make us," he said. "Then they tell stories about us that aren't real. 'Cause they love us, right? That's what they say." He added without rancor, "They love us to death. They make us up and then they make us believe it and then we do the rest. We do it. Us. Not like your Jewish doctor. I tell you the story of Wolf?"

He had. He would again. Every time he told me, the story changed or I changed, or Grandfather, as unlikely as that seemed to his grandson, changed.

"One time, Wolf come through the forest looking to hide. Bear helped him capture Elk and Wolf tricked him and stole the carcass. He cut himself skinning the Elk he stole from Bear and he licked where he was cut and this Wolf liked the taste of his blood so much that he began to eat himself. He was hungry, you know. It was winter and he couldn't stop eat-

ing himself, so he was going through the woods looking for
ways to hide because if he didn't stop eating himself soon he
would eat himself all up. Then he would need Coyote to help
him bring him back to life. Wolf didn't like Coyote much, you
see, 'cause Coyote was so much like him that at a little ways you
can hardly tell Coyote from Wolf. So Wolf, he runs through
the forest. He tries to hide beneath the fir trees, but Snowbird sees him. 'Wolf,' Snowbird says, 'What are you doing
there beneath the fir trees?' and Wolf, he says to Snowbird,
'I'm not Wolf,' and he takes a bite out of himself and as he is
chewing, Snowbird laughs at him and says, 'Sure you are
Wolf and you are eating yourself all up.' Well, with that, Wolf
runs away. He goes down to the river and Badger sees him
and calls to him, 'Wolf, why are you eating yourself behind
those rocks there?' and Wolf says, 'I'm not Wolf,' and Badger
laughs at him, 'Sure you are Wolf.' Well, that Wolf he doesn't
know what to do, so he decides to change his name. Wolf decides to add an extra letter to his name, two effs, he decides,
then I will stop eating Wolf and I will be eating Wolff instead.
Well, Ollokot (Frog) put his head up and he sees Wolf-Two-
Effs eating and eating himself and he knows Wolf cannot
stop so he swims the river to get Coyote. 'Wolf is eating himself up again,' Ollokot told to Coyote. Coyote, he doesn't forget, but he doesn't remember until Wolf tricked him with the
Elk. 'I asked Wolf for help,' Coyote said. 'He's greedy and
eats himself all up and I helped him and helped him and I
ask him to help me. Remember?' Coyote was sick and asked
Wolf to help him and Wolf, he said he was busy. He would
save his help for Badger or Fox, not waste it with Coyote. But
Coyote knew how much they were alike, him and Wolf, even
though Wolf grew fat eating himself all the time. So when
Ollokot said come, Coyote just said to him why should I?

'Hurry,' said Ollokot. 'He has changed his name to Wolff.' So Coyote went with Frog to the place beside Badger's river and found Wolf's jaws which were all that was left of Wolf. He took the jaws and buried them. Then he stepped over them five times the way Fox taught him and he brought Wolf back to the world. Even if Wolf sewed on three effs to his name, Coyote would always bring him back to the world, 'cause Coyote knew they were brothers.

"That made Wolf real angry and afraid that Coyote should know their likeness, but it only made Coyote laugh. He didn't want to be like Wolf either. But without Wolf, who would know?"

II

The story of Wolf and Coyote, made up as it was by Grandfather out of the gumbo of experience or necessity, remains for me a pleasant story, entertaining as well as instructive. Even though I knew that Grandfather told stories not to escape but to describe what was real, the reality it told seemed when I was young little more than a lesson in being myself. I did not suspect that the experience behind it, the experience that directly or indirectly was necessary for the proper telling of it, might be Grandfather's own or that it was tinged with a bitterness that he did not want me or my sisters to inherit. Underneath the tale was a longer something and it was a something that his fabling, much like his laughter, was meant to disguise, if not to hide. It was not an ineffable something. Rather, it was ineffable to someone like me who, at the time, lacked either the foresight which is wisdom or the experience to fable it.

What strikes me about Grandfather's stories was how they lacked what my teachers called "verb tense." By tense, they meant, of course, grammar, which is a way not only to organize ideas but also time, giving those ideas a past or a future. They had taught me grammar and time the way Grandfather's brothers and sisters had been adopted into white families and taught how to dress and pray. Grammar was the dress and prayer was the time, and I was already learning how to talk about the past and hope for the future while ignoring the real that Grandfather told. Partly, it was the way he told it – as story or tale, with a lesson to be learned only if you were willing to listen as much to what was not said, which requires a kind of mature awareness that may explain why enjoying Henry James was a product of age to my sister, who told her brother, lost on his search for clarity in James, that perhaps he needed to be older – thirty, say – to truly enjoy *The Golden Bowl*. Without the mature awareness either for James or for what wasn't said by Grandfather, I never imagined that Grandfather meant to lack consistent tense. And as arrogant as youth can be, I often was too busy silently grading his grammar to pay real attention and see what he was giving me – an awareness of the possibility that all these ideas and beliefs organized by the grammar of time and tense were only half-truths, plots without story, the heard-told without the unheard-unsaid.

   . . .

Schooling, the process by which I was learning to listen selectively or to not listen at all, was one of the plots, and I managed to do okay at it, although not as well as my older sisters whose imaged successes were held up to me by teachers who wanted me to behave like them. The more I learned to ignore, the better I did, although papers for English and History remained a problem for me because in English I wanted every paper to be the story of an idea and not its explication, and History seemed too easy and sure of itself to be true. Lab reports were the most difficult, however, except the one time I faked a result in Chemistry, getting a white precipitate by pinching laundry detergent into my test tube which so excited my teacher, Mr. Iverson, that I was too ashamed to point out the box of Fab on the shelf right in front of us. My little joke turned sour in the sheer frisson of his excitement, and as a self-inflicted punishment, I spent a week inventing a lab report filled with an excitement to equal his. I did not have the courage to attempt to reproduce my precipitate success for interested parents on the night of Open House. Nor did I have the strength to refuse Mr. Iverson's invitation to perform. More than old enough now to enjoy *The Golden Bowl*, I am still ashamed that on the night of Open House, I simply failed to show up, explaining later that I'd gotten the time wrong, letting Mr. Iverson do what he would with whatever concepts he had of Indian time. For me, at that age, Indian time was nothing more than an excuse. Better, I thought, that Mr. Iverson have a gap in his laboratorious demonstrations than to have to tell him that all his excitement was for nothing.

Perhaps it was that shame and excuse that made me become obsessed with responsibility that year. When Gigi Tincher complained in English to Mr. Breault that "we" already had too much homework and did we have to read so much of *Tale of Two Cities* and Mr. Breault looked down at his desk and said, "Well maybe I could. . . ," I could not resist asking Gigi if she would kindly resist whining and just do – or not do – the work and take responsibility for that. Other students agreed – Gigi complained in every class, in every week, that the life of her schooling was burdensome – but it came as no surprise that Mr. Breault, with his crush on the fair Gigi, turned against me for my rudeness. It did come as a surprise that he baldly asked me to leave the classroom and go outside, and when I asked where I would sit because the grass was wet, he roundly suggested I might want to take along my desk, which, with a good deal of commotion, I did, picking up the chair and desktop screwed to an aluminum tubular frame and wedging it through the door. I put it in the middle of a lawn, on the rise of a small Yahi mound and, the times being permissive and my school in stocks with the time, day after day I sat outside and read stories or stared into the California sky looking for clouds, waiting for rain, or deciding where aircraft passing overhead were going and dreaming up the lives of the folks on board, an infinitely progressive invention. It was there, staring up at a sky as clear as Saran Wrap, that I began to hear the tenses that Grandfather purposely lacked and to feel the difference in time, or sense of it, that his grammar described. The time of my schooling was like the emperor's clothes to the time he inhabited and, striving to please my teachers, good men and women who meant so well, I had come to resemble someone akin to the emperor. Their grammar was useful for organizing ideas and falsifying lab reports. But when telling stories, it wasn't necessary and it wasn't necessarily true. It was out of a different kind of time, a time in which the tenses of grammar boil together like camas roots, that Grandfather borrowed his tales. I saw that, there at my desk on the mound. For weeks, thinking bad grammar would bring me into synch with Grandfather's time, I went around saying, "Ain't," or using double negatives – "Don't make no difference" – until Father grew weary of not listening to me and decided it did.

Schooling aged me, but because of Grandfather's dreaming, because of his stories, deep down I came to believe that everything true was story, something to be told or said which was true for the saying. My own stories were not always good, though, and more than one girlfriend said what my wife has sometimes said and the look on her face still sometimes says: "Blah, blah, blah." More important, sitting outside Mr. Breault's class and no doubt influenced by the recitals of the successes of my sisters, I took up reading. I got to fall in love with books, especially books that told stories. Again because of Grandfather, all that mattered to me was whether or not the stories were told, which was the same as true. Books for me remained stories through the firestorm of the sixties, the consolidation of the seventies, and the dogged capitalism of the eighties, and who told the story mattered less than how well it was told.

   . . .

There would come a time when I wanted to believe that only Indians can write authentically about Indians, but my mixblood reminded me to not be so sure. As N. Scott Momaday has said, it cuts both ways. The non-Indian writer may write well about the Indian and the Indian about the non. And though it does seem odd, initially, that Oklahoma's American Indian Literature and Critical Studies publication series might want to publish a novel by a non-Indian, albeit a non-Indian who has devoted much of his scholarly life to the effort to load Indian literature into the American canon, the idea of it seems peculiarly liberating from the kind of determinations being used to describe just what American Indian literature is.

One thing it is not — and this seems obvious — is homogeneous, although there are plenty of people who would homogenize it. Outside of Gerald Vizenor, who has remained remarkably free in his work, few Indians, mixblood or full, ever get published by editors who think all books should be like all other books, and the image of the mixblood writer or artist who is pressured to make his (or her) work look like all other art crops up not only in the stories but also in the lives-as-writers of mixblood artists. These pressures for recognizable homogeneity don't simply come from one side; they come from Indian writers and critics, as well.[1] But, despite the current romanticized love affair with all things Indian, the vast majority of editors (and, I might add, art dealers) seem to not always take the time to ask themselves if they are publishing Indian writers because they are fashionably Indian or because they truly tell stories in any particularly Indian way. With the filtering system of mainstream literary agents, it seems as though very few American Indian writers get published unless they put the emperor's clothes on their prose, which can make their stories as inauthentic as Wolf with two effs. Even the recent production of Indian novels — many of which are wonderful stories — risks passing as quick as love turns back to hate unless critics continue to tell how the Indian novel belongs in the commonly accepted group that gets called, among other things, the canon.[2]

Even if critics do that, there remains the problem of authenticity and seriousness. To prove that he (or she) is both serious (or worth taking seriously) and authentic — really Indian writing about real things or really writing about Indian things or some mixture of the two — he may become as solemn as nails and give up the humor (serious or laughing) about himself that allows him to survive. That allowed Grandfather to survive. Humor is necessary, yet he may give up the trickster humor of Coyote and eat himself up like Wolf. In other words, he may begin to "do" broccoli.

Trickster humor often tricks the self and in that tricking, forces the ego to know or realize something of the place of that self in the communal, enduring world of selves. Coyote humor often negates or at least submerges the ego; the humor is performed for, but also by, the participants in any individual tale of Coyote. Without this kind of humor, Coyote becomes merely clever and while what he does may be funny, it is filled with so much ego that he falls in love with it and falling in love, he begins to consume himself.

At least part of the humor – and I mean it as an attitude, a position of the self in relation, not simply as hah-hah laughter – of both Coyote (or Fox) as well as grandfather comes from the humorous self's sense of acting out his life against an ongoing background of Time (or Fate). Thus, to give up his humor may mean more than egotistically devouring himself (and there is no dreaming way I know of to blame this devouring on anyone but the self). It may also mean giving up his sense of and his harmony with time and, consequently, meaning. This can put the Indian writer into a kind of inward spiral and the more humorless he (or she) becomes, although it may be more salable, the less meaning he has. Losing his humor could result in his becoming a point on the non-Indian line of Manifest Destiny, a point which may be passed over neatly as soon as the movie gets made.

Then there is an opposite problem, especially for the mixblood who does not look darkly Lakota or Navaho, which arises if you do not constantly and publicly present yourself as Indian. Some of us – shy by nature – have learned to be a little shy about this Indian stuff; because we don't wear feathers, our friends feel free to laugh at our mention of it or to denigrate the contributions of Indians to "culture," and feeling slightly angry and slightly confused, we keep a lot of it to ourselves. If we reveal our anger, they snap, "How much Indian are you, anyway?"

"How much effing stupid are you?" someone must be tempted to ask.

One of my colleagues once said that being black was serious but being Indian was "more like a hobby."

Well, paint my face.

. . .

Having heard these things and worse, which is what gave his humor that undercurrent of sorrow and sometime bitterness, Grandfather believed in school, so school I did. He said to study, especially (their) stories; he said if he had, he would have known. What he would have known was left up to me. But he said that if I told stories, to tell them the way they had to be told. How would I know that?

"They'll let you know," he said.

Although it took me some years to finish school, dropping in and out whenever the love of unstoried talk (which some call meetings or conferences if they want to make you attend to it) overwhelmed my sense of the world, I did. I learned to love Homer's Penelope not because she was other but because she was faithful like Grandmother, who also complained a little and often in her challenges to Grandfather. When Odysseus cleared his lodge of that bunch of talkers, I cheered the aim of those lances and each feathered arrow. I felt the honor of the cycling heroes Telemachus and Odysseus as they took away the suitors' nightmare and ended that interminable conference in the Great Hall. All stories had in them right and wrong. They meant something, and if they didn't they are wrong.

"But how do you prove it?" people asked.

My heart knew. But if I said that, someone could call me an "ist" — essentialist or racist. Perhaps by "heart" I should mean some metaphor for a feeling kind of knowing and yet, while it is in part describable as a feeling kind of knowing, it is much more than that – and it is no metaphor. It is connection. Perhaps it may be called the dreaming heart – a heart which, in the activity of opening itself to possibility, recognizes, wants, invents a willing dialogue with more than the (limited) self. It is not mind, in the Western sense of rational, pragmatical, or logical thinking; perhaps it is landscape, a ground to which the Dreamer is connected and out of which comes his voice for speaking or telling, once the land has been lost. It definitely is story, a story of and by the heart, and if any of it is true or told right, you know. In your heart, if nowhere else. For the heart is the chamber where ideas run into each other, talk things over, have a drink or a smoke, and leave, willing to be wrong.

So although it is possible to know with the heart if you're Nez Perce or Osage, teachers and friends who are not want the same thing I demand of my students: evidence, analysis, explanation. Some of my friends want evidence they can disprove because they want, ultimately, all things to be equal; otherwise they fear that what they do won't or doesn't matter. I know in my heart that what I *do* may not matter; if it's told well, though, the fact that it may not doesn't matter. My heart is satisfied.

"Pah!" they may say. "How can you be sure of that."

"Because I have a heart," I have to say.

But nowadays it seems as though everyone has an equal heart, and soul may be eaten in Harlem, and no one knows anything for sure and that's why Hey! if some pathetic white guy wants to drum his way to spirituality, it's his privilege, and environmentalists are fools because the earth won't end only people, and I have to say, "But the earth is heart and its people are the heart's body and without Human Beings it may as well be a lump of rock drifting through a snow-cold universe. . . ."

"Here he goes," they are required to say, winking at an auditory friend, real or imagined, and I want to let fly with a quiver of house-clearing arrows.

. . .

The story of heart is also a story of time. When I began to study their stories, Claude Lévi-Strauss was tucking himself into the critical canon. I thought about entropy and structural syntheses with my heart, took up the expected words and grammar (I pinned a hermeneutical lexicon over my desk) and wrote articles that would make Frog yawn. Because of Grandfather's stories, I knew that Time was more than a structure imposed upon stories. Time, the sense of it, in a sense, had to do with everything – with knowing, dreaming, feeling, laughing – even surviving broccoli. A person's response to time and Time reveals the possibilities as well as the dangers and, in both a direct and a roundabout way, it highlights some of the problems of being or becoming a mixblood writer (and most of the Indian writers currently publishing are mixblood) who not only writes in the midst of the production of American literature but who has adopted (must adopt?) the grammar and tenseful uses of time, the language, and even some of the forms of the dominant storytelling culture. Here, Grandfather is clear, and each morning before dawn as I remember him and myself in relation to him, an act akin to dreaming before I get to work, he reminds me that my time – not just my sense of it, but its passage as well – is different. But what is it different from? And why does my daughter ask on long drives not, "How much longer?" but, "Daddy, why do we always arrive in the dark?"

III

Nothing tempts me more than to say that Time does not exist. But of course it does, even if it is a construct as simple as telling a five-year-old to count to sixty four hundred and eighty times and we'll be there. Listening to her labor through ten or twelve of these numerations is not only a linear burden but, as she begins with the number one yet again, a circular one as well. In the circle is a trust, a willingness to believe in Daddy, an innocence, perhaps, but an innocence that turns sophisticated just at the moment you conclude its childishness and arrive in the dark.

Anyone who took up smoking as a way to measure out his time at work knows that time on the clock not only exists, but it's a killer. If he gives up smoking, he finds that he has nothing but time on his hands – time to think about too many things, time to feel dull, time to hang out with his coworkers, and time especially to listen to their stories. For everybody has them, stories, although the times I've had too much time on my hands and listened to some of theirs, I've felt embarrassed by what their stories reveal, by the narrowness of their time and their personal nature. The intimacy of these stories ranges from sexual quirks to habits of toiletry to psychological injury or weakness to attitudes towards other people that no one should admit to having. I am as uncomfortable when a relative stranger tells me that without constipating drugs his wife would've had a messy time of his bed-ridden recuperation as I am when some other stranger (or perhaps the same one) begins to explicate the problems in his sex life. This is not the response to impropriety that many people call WASP-ishness, by which they seem to mean a kind of cool, aristocratic aloofness and privacy; it is simple embarrassment. I can be as improper as the next person, but the details of my individual life (like my imagination) remain mine and mine alone, to be revealed to strangers and familiars alike only as the seeds of narrative, told to illustrate or illuminate something beyond me, aimed at bringing a meaning out of the relation of the parts to the whole, and thus usually or almost always modified or transformed like Coyote or Bear. Details, or some of them anyway, seem unimportant unless they are in relation to reveal.

Confessional or private revelations of detail seem pinpoint small, even insignificant on a broadly human scale, and in their way, limited in the tenses used to convey them. The grammatical construct – tense – used to organize the temporal construct – chronological time – is usually limited to the narrative past or, more often, the present tense. The broad-based, large-visioned reflexivity of self to selves increasingly seems to be lost. In large part, this lost reflexivity, this image of a collective self expressed or represented by the individual self (or his individualized allegory of his culture or society) is something that, if Arnold Krupat is correct, has not been "much present in the West since perhaps the sixteenth century" (Krupat, 134).[3]

By this, I don't mean to not say that the West in which and of which Grandfather made Father, my sisters, and me by leaving Indian Territory for Los Angeles, the city of mixed blood – lacks all relation of time to Time, although it does seem that here-and-now detail and a thin facticity increasingly substitute for analogic meaning and ambiguous (or open) dialogue, that the tenses of Western, and specifically North American, narrative prose are shrinking towards the dominant present tense, as the sense of time telescopes closed and its cycles seem to approximate the cycles of fashion, and that the lives of characters become increasingly that, the lives of characters who are interesting not because they have depth or wisdom or flaws of tragic proportions but because they are perceived as quirky, odd, or marginal. What I *am* saying is that a lot of contemporary Western storytelling seems to lack the relations that Native American storytelling demands.

Even though *in* the West, and indeed, at least partly *of* it, this reflexivity and relation of tenses and "times" was never lost by Grandfather. The stories he told, broader-based and less day-to-day tales with more generalized or representative details, were without past or future, plu- or future-perfect tense. Though he used English, and thus had to use tenses in one way or another, the consistency of tense was not important because there was no real "now" or "then" to the meaning of his stories but more of an "always." Wolf was Wolf, Coyote Coyote; when one heard, he began to hear the understanding of the illusions that seem to attend upon a too-great insistence on the efficacy of time, much the way we go for walks and my daughter listens to stories about Snowbird and gradually – noticeable in the moments she begins to make up her own tales of Snowbird or Badger or the other figures that populate our walking – she comes to see herself as related directly to Snowbird, a self in relation to a self to which all other clever (cleverness is one of Snowbird's characteristics) selves are related. Even though the stories about Snowbird have a point and several contextually possible meanings, similar to grandfather's stories about Wolf-Two-Effs, the main reason for the stories, as I see them, is to teach that "always," that "durance" and "survivance" (as Gerald Vizenor calls them) that comes from a narrative sense of the tenseless all-time of knowing.

. . .

"Long ago there was Bird," Rachel says. She grins, a quiet

grin aimed inwards – though she knows I see it – a shy grin, hoping and knowing at the same time.

"What was Mr. Bird like?"

"He's yellow. He was color."

I don't correct her grammar because she's only five. Well, truthfully, age has nothing to do with it. It's the echo of something past that pleases. "Okay, so long ago there was Yellow Bird."

"Uh-huh." It's fall and cool and Rachel and I are on our way to the park where she will play with friends or, as sometimes she does, play alone in a crowd of kids with Daddy for audience. Her baby brother, who loves being outdoors, vocalizes in his stroller, singing private songs to the shadows of birds and leaves or growling like the hydraulics of a garbage truck. Stuart scrabbles up a tree – all squirrels are named "Stuart" to Rachel unless they are black and then they're Stuart's cousin. Stuart really gets around, let me tell you, and the Stuart hunting about for storage as we pass him does not seem fat enough, ready for winter, which Rachel takes to mean that winter isn't coming. Not for a while, anyway.

"What did Yellow Bird do?"

"Told stories."

"What kind of stories?"

"The kind . . . [she pauses, hunting about for words] about things."

"Things?"

She's suddenly tired. Or else she knows that she's gotten far enough along that she can say, "Daddy, I don't feel like telling a story. You tell me one."

"Really? Okay," I say, wondering if I've been tricked and who has done the tricking. I don't feel any more like telling a story than she does; but I couldn't help but ask questions as soon as she said "Long ago." Now I'm stuck.

"Look! Stuart's cousin!"

"Yep. Looks like it." I quit long ago arguing that there was more than one brown squirrel in the world. "Okay, how do all stories start?"

"Once upon a time," we say in unison.

I go on, making it as I go, determined to summon the energy to finish. Just that afternoon I'd gotten a rejection letter from a magazine saying that my piece seemed cold and detached; it wasn't the rejection that bothered me but the demand for adverbial involvement, and it made me weary.

"Okay. There was Badger. Badger could see in the dark, like Owl, and when he saw Snowbird or Hare, Snake or Elk, he liked to stop and tell them a story about what he saw in the dark. They listened politely to him for many years. But one day they began to turn away from him. 'Hey, Hare. The other day I saw a trap. . . ,' Badger would say. 'That's nice,' Hare would say, and off he'd go without hearing the end of the story. 'Did I ever tell you about the men in plaid coats and bright orange hats?' he'd begin to Elk. 'Ummm,' Elk would reply, munching a munch of brush thoughtfully before edging away.

"Well, you would think that this would make Badger angry," I say to Rachel who has stopped and bent towards lichen on the roots of an oak. She pokes it, tilts her head at it, and then looks up, apologetic.

I grin at her. "But it didn't. No, it didn't make Badger angry that his friends couldn't listen. It made him sorry. But he couldn't stop telling them when he saw them, and before too long, he began to laugh a little when he told things, not because he thought it was funny but because he didn't want them to feel bad for not listening, and a little laugh went a long ways for that.

"'Hey, Snowbird,' he'd say, and laugh, as though to say, Okay, fly away now 'cause otherwise I'll have to tell you things.

"He laughed more and more, until at last a sly grin was stuck to his snout like the one Bear wears just before he growls. 'Hey, Badger,' Coyote said to him, 'you're looking a lot like Bear, these days,' and that Badger, he thought, why not? If I were Bear, I wouldn't be Badgering my friends all the time with stuff I see in the dark, and he says, 'Coyote, Coyote, teach me to be Bear, can you do that?'

"Well, that Coyote, he can do that, but he says, 'You don't want to be Bear. Bear smells worse than Skunk. The way he body-burps all the time you can tell what he had for lunch if you cross his picnic two hours after it's over.' 'I don't care,' Badger says. 'Teach me to be Bear. Can you do that?' 'I can do that,' Coyote says. 'Close your eyes and do what I say.'

"So Badger, he closes his eyes. 'Stand on your hind legs and wave your paws at me,' Coyote says, and Badger manages to stand on his hind legs and wave his paws. 'Good,' Coyote says, beginning to enjoy this. 'Now open your mouth and sound like a garbage truck, only louder, like you expect me to be scared.' And Badger did that. 'Okay,' Coyote says, laughing, 'Now get down on all fours and squeeze your stomach in and out and burp out your butt.' And Badger did that, too. 'Louder,' Coyote said, and Badger, he body-burped so loud that Junco fled from the trees above them. 'Okay,' Coyote said, holding his laughter in, 'You're Bear, now.'

"Well Badger was so pleased that he ran to Snowbird. 'Hey, Snowbird,' he said, and before she could turn away, 'Fffffwwitt!' He sneaked up behind Owl. 'Ffffwaaapp!' he went, causing Owl to start and say, 'Who?' Here and there he went, burping at his friends, and when he came to some fishermen he burped so loud that they ran away and left their catch of Salmon and that Badger he had himself a picnic then and for a week after the whole forest smelled like a campground latrine.

"Finally, though, winter came. Badger soon grew tired of staying in his den and pretending to sleep. He was hungry. The den smelled from his burping, and all he wanted to do was go out and tell someone something, anything, as long as it was telling. He wanted just to be Badger again. Well, why not? he thought one day, and he crawled out to look for Snowbird or Hare. He looked high and he looked low. When he finally found Snowbird, he said, 'Snowbird, will you listen to me?' but Snowbird said, 'Ugh, I don't listen to you, Bear.' 'It's Badger,' he said. 'You sure look all fat and furry to me,' Snowbird said. 'Like Bear.' So Badger crawled off to find Hare. Well, he found Hare – and Deer and Salmon and Elk and Junco – but they all said the same thing. Their friend Badger had gone and left them without knowing what you could see in the dark. 'I'm Badger,' Badger said. 'Your friend.' But Elk only turned to Hare and shook his horns. 'It's only Bear trying to trick us,' and they all walked away in their directions.

"Badger, he blamed Coyote. 'That darned Coyote,' he said, 'He tricked me.'

"Finally, he came to Wolf's den. Wolf was out, but her cubs were home. Badger poked his head in. 'Who're you?' a cub asked. 'Buh . . . buh . . . Badger,' he said. 'He looks like Bear,' another cub said. 'Badger,' Badger said. 'Okay,' the first cub said, 'prove it.' 'How?' Badger asked. 'Badger us what you see in the dark,' the second cub says, 'That's what Momma says you do.' 'Okay. Okay,' Badger replied, trying to remember something he once saw in the dark. He thought and he thought and then he cleared his throat. It sounded like a growl. The cubs were afraid. 'It's okay,' Badger told the cubs, 'it's just a bad habit I have.' Well, Badger then got up on his hind legs and waved his paws and tried to begin telling them something to prove he was Badger and not Bear, but nothing would come out. He opened his mouth wider. Nothing. He tried to push the words out. Still nothing. Finally, he got down on all fours and pushed and pushed and all of a sudden, 'Fffffwwwwaaapppp!'

"Here's the park," I say. "Where do you want to start, the swings?"

"But Daddy, what happened?"

"I'll tell you later," I say. She accepts this. When she's older, she'll suspect that I don't know what happens. Younger or older, she'll be able – if she wants – to count on one thing, and that's that she or I will tell this story again, at least in part because it's not a particularly well-told one. Not yet. It may become a good one as she or I retell it, adding to it, modifying it, improving it. I try to listen over the story's objections to the way I've told it for the story to let me know how it needed to be told. As I watch her lope off towards the swings, following behind at a distance, I hear the echo of Grandfather telling me to tell something again, and again, making me repeat the process over and over until I understood. The important first thing is the telling (the way of telling becomes important only later, after a good deal of self-awareness has set in, after, indeed, one has tried to be Bear and failed). Identity comes later, discovered in the connection provided by the telling or re-invented as a result of discovering and telling the connection.

IV

Even if someone might be tempted to ascribe Grandfather's grammar to the fact that he had only three years of schooling as a welder at the Haskell Indian Institute, he'd be wrong. Grandfather's stories were without tense because Grandfather is without tense. The kind of individualized, bourgeois time the teachers tried to teach him at Haskell was foreign to him. Were he to tell the story of the flight of the nontreaty Nez Perce,[4] stopping to point to where Joseph's lodge was by the three pines or where Ollokot and Yellow Bird pitched theirs, offering the encounters between Joseph or Ollokot and General Howard the way Homer offers the encounter of Achilles's shade with the harrowing Odysseus, the story's elements and form would begin to become familiar to non-Indian listeners and readers. Both stories are capable of being retold with greater or lesser modification, though necessarily with some; if the interest or imaginative involvement of the storyteller remains high, he is going to alter some details and imagine new ones, if only to meet the demands of a shifting context. Both would be considered highly oral, and both could be described as coming out of a significant oral tradition. The fact that Homer's was the younger oral tradition would not have bothered Grandfather at all. He could appreciate a good story; he would expect Homer to appreciate his.

The similarities in the two oral traditions – indeed, among all oral traditions, including, for example, the one Amos Tutuola writes out of – have been fairly documented. The story of the *Odyssey* uses time in the same way Grandfather might. Against the background of ongoing, unspecified time are set the journeys of Odysseus and Telemachus. One, the Nostoi, is the journey of Odysseus home, the first journey-quest he must endure for Poseidon's need to revenge himself on the hero who blinded his son *and* had the gall or stupidity to give up his anonymity and to shout his name at the stone-throwing Polyphemus, a moment of speaking his identity in defiance and arrogance which has disastrous consequences for his crew as well as himself. Arnold Krupat suggests in *The Voice in the Margin* that the chronology of telling stories beginning with the protagonist's birth and aiming like an arrow at his death, giving the background of the subject's early life, is a Western concept of autobiographical storytelling structure, not an Indian one. I wonder – though the *Odyssey* is not autobiography – if the opposition or division is less "Western/Eastern" and more "oral/less oral" and if this difference does not suggest something important: namely, that Indian autobiography resembles in structure Greek epic, and the Indian autobiographer creates a relation in which the individual's day-to-day life is not what's important, but the representative individual's life in relation to the established history or background of his people is. And further that when the Indian storyteller departs from autobiography into fiction, if he (or she) doesn't carry this almost-anonymous, ego-submerged-in-relation sense of telling with him and thus even in the other forms of his prose, linear chronology is as unimportant (and perhaps as false) as representational realism.

Even the story of Telemachus's coming-of-age begins with a dream-vision as he is sent in his twenty-first year on a quest for news of his father, a quest which both allows him to and proves that he can grow up, come into his own as a young man with superior qualities of loyalty, bravery, courage, foresight, and skill to reach a level of stature similar to his father's before he returns home. There are no long sections describing Telemachus's birth or childhood; rather the individualized chronology is denied in favor of the relation of present events with the background of cultural or Ithakan history. This denial creates the sense that this story is beginning in the middle of things, a beginning similar in structure to the one Krupat takes note of in the *Life of Black Hawk* where Black Hawk begins his "autobiography" with the place and date of his birth and then "shifts immediately to a story about a prophecy to his great-grandfather of the coming of the white man" (Krupat 1989, 152), a kind of beginning in the middle of meaning, if not things. Granted that *Black Hawk* is autobiography and the *Odyssey* is not, but it does suggest a similarity of structural function: the cultural autobiography, if I may call it that, of the *Odyssey* is tied by the temporal structure into the same background and leads the listener-reader into the same Time as the poet or recorder; the personal autobiography, which is not personal at all, links the reader by means of unrealistic story "specifically to the history of the Sauk-and-Fox encounters with the French and the British" (Krupat 1989, 152). How much or how truly Black Hawk's story does this, Krupat reminds us, cannot be determined fully because of the editorial interference of J. B. Patterson who followed – as editors of autobiography up to the present do – a "Chronological Imperative." Indian autobiography and, I would maintain, Indian storytelling and all storytelling that remains bound to an oral tradition (again, Tutuola is an adequate example) disrupts this imperative, tells stories that are not "linear or temporally sequential," freely digresses dialogically in what I call "supplementation," and uses voices within the narrative that may not be labeled realistic but which may be called transformationally representational – among other things.

    . . .

Stories – all stories handed down or made anew – like people get their meaning from reflection on the past and the connection with tradition and in Native America that tradition remains oral. Indeed, stories are the way or mode of reflection and when Rachel and I make one up together, it is less the story that matters and more the making itself, the processional making of the understanding of the connection. At her age, the process ties her into the time of her father and her father into her grammar-free newness and joy. If she tells her children the same stories in fifteen or twenty years, she will be doing something else, acting not only to preserve the times we've had and the sense of them but also the connections her father felt with his father and all the grandmothers and fathers before. To do this, she will have to abandon the comforts of representational realism, what Gerald Vizenor (quoting David Carroll) calls the "monologic realism" which is a "'bureaucratic solution' to neocolonialism" (Vizenor 1993, 6), as well as any chronological imperative she may feel. She may do something as simple as let the voices of dead persons speak, or even make Death a character in the narrative. Or she may draw upon the line breaks of poetry, use extreme indirection and dislocation, or even repeat whole sections – if not the whole itself – of the story as a commentary on how hearing the story creates the significance of past actions, as Karl Kroeber suggests happens in *The Golden Woman* (Vizenor 1993, 30).

Like Homer's daughter (if it was Homer's daughter) she may even retell fables like Scylla or Charybdis or supplementations like the listing of underworld heroes in their entirety, perhaps modifying them according to the context of the interior listeners (in the Homeric, Penelope, but in the Rachelic, perhaps Snowbird or Bear) but not so much, waiting to shorten the repeated segments to a few lines that essentially say, "Odysseus, the master storyteller, told Penelope all that had happened since the fall of Troy," until the moment she writes it all down, records it, shapes it, edits it – as Homer's daughter may well have done. One of her instincts, like Grandfather's or for that matter, mine, drawn from the connection which is a part of the oral tradition or the oral necessity of telling a story, is to preserve – names, customs, events, attitudes – and thus the self-conscious suggestion by the faithful swineherd that Odysseus's fables are lies told for a night's lodging or transportation home seems to become an indicator of the distance between the preserver and what is to be preserved. At the moment she decides, as the narrator of Heinrich Böll's "Seventh Trunk" so simply says about the so-complicated process, to "write it all down," she faces a very real problem, whether she is conscious of it or not: how does she preserve that which she wants to preserve in written language, which is so much less fluid and which requires fewer rhetorical acts like extreme and lengthy repetitions – since it may be reread – than the original form of the story? And, if I may use Homer's daughter to speculatively make a point, what if she decides to "write it all down" in English and not Greek or, in her case, Osage or Nez Perce?

It is a problem with which monolingual Rachel is not faced, directly or immediately, though indirectly and eventually a question she will want to consider if she chooses to tell stories to her children or to strangers, if she wants to avoid opening her stories to "dim-witted misunderstanding" (Vizenor 1993, 19). Once she finds a way to tell what is real, she'll have to find her own voice. Beneath my tales are my experiences – some of them hurtful or bitter – which I have *let* her ignore just the way Grandfather let me ignore the unheard-unsaid long ago for two reasons: I don't want her to inherit my hurts; and telling the tales, finding a way to say them, bridges the gap between her and not Grandfather's experiences but his spirit which is in the saying. The *act* of telling builds that bridge, fortifies it and, later – when she has her own experiences, some of which must needs be bitter – defends it.

The rest is up to her. How will she let the voices of the dead speak when from the beginning they have spoken to her in a tongue that was foreign to them? What tenses will she pitch? If she writes it down, what dangers await her like Scylla and Charybdis, Badger and Bear, and dare she admit these dangers to her readerly crew as they row her past them?

5

SCYLLA OR THE TRUE SPELLING OF MOURNING

Once there was Brook. He was thin and clear and lived high in the Wallowa Mountains with Elk and Bear and the Human Beings. He loved to sing. He sang as he twisted and turned slowly through the forest over stones and under the hooves of Elk. He sang because he liked to sing and he liked the Human Beings who came to cup their hands and drink up his pure singing. One day Brook was humming along when he came to a rock that was not there before. The rock was large, a boulder. It blocked his way. Brook felt himself starting to pool so he pushed and pushed at Rock and Rock refused to move. Brook was afraid. He saw Frog. Frog was asleep in a shaft of sun on a fallen branch sticking out from the bank. Frog loved Brook. Frog said Brook was his best friend. Frog, Brook sang, help me. Help me move this rock. After, I will let you swim with me. Frog, he thought, Brook is my friend. I will help him for his letting me swim in him yesterday and the many days before. So Frog, he hopped over and helped Brook push and push at Rock. Rock barely budged but Brook felt Rock's budging and he thought Now I will have to let Frog swim in my clear waters. I will be stuck with him all day. Try lower down, Brook said to Frog. I'll push up here and together we will move Rock. Frog dove beneath the clear water and pushed at Rock's feet. He pushed and pushed, and at last Rock tumbled over once. Out of breath from so much pushing he kicked to the surface. Brook, he said, whew. But Brook was nowhere to be seen. You know that Brook, he had rushed on and hidden himself in Stream. Oh well, Frog thinks, he probably forgot his words, and feeling hungry from his work, he swam off to hunt for flies. The sun ended that day and the next and Frog forgot Brook's broken words. On the third day, Frog was floating along, minding his own business and keeping his eye out for Water Walkers and flies. He heard a strange singing. He went to see. The strange singing was coming from Stream. Stream, said Frog, what is wrong with your voice? And Stream said, It is my cousin Brook. You hear how he sings? He's been staying with me for three days. Brook looked out and saw Frog. Hey-uh, Brook said. I thought you had become lost. What happened? When I came up you were. . . , Frog began. He wanted to explain. He did not know yet if it was necessary. I saved you these, Brook interrupted. He gave Frog flies, still living, caught in a floating spider's web. Frog was happy. He was very happy that his friend brought him such gifts. Thank you, Frog said, ashamed that he ever thought that Brook had sneaked off on purpose. Frog accepted Brook's gift. He ate the flies, and fell asleep to the strange harmony of Brook and Stream singing together. When he woke, the singing was stopped and Stream was sad. Stream, Frog said, why are you silent? Brook left, Stream said. In the middle of a spirit song. The sun ended that day and the next. On the third day, Frog was hopping along the floor of the valley. He came to Pool where he heard singing. Low and soft, the singing was, as though the singer sang beneath his blanket. It was Brook. Brook was singing softly. His pure voice was muted by the still deep waters in Pool. It was sad singing that made Frog's heart heavy. He sat on the edge of the pool. He waited for night to come to the mountains. He saw Brook in the moon's light. Why are you sad? Frog asked Brook. You who used to sing a happy song. I am stuck in this Pool, Brook whispered. It is dark and warm. Help me, Brook told Frog in the darkness. I gave you those flies. You are my best friend, Frog said. I will help you because I love your singing. But I thank you for the generous gift flies, too. What do I do? Frog asked. Pool has me caught, Brook answered. But if there were a hole in Beaver's dam I could seep through it. Can you make a hole like that? Yes, Frog said. I will do it. Frog dove beneath the still water. He turned his back to Beaver's dam and kicked. He kicked and he kicked. It hurt his feet to kick and yet Frog rose to the air, swallowed, and returned to his kicking. The wall of Beaver's dam grew thin. Are you ready? he asked Brook. I am ready, Brook said, and before Frog dived for the kicks that would break Beaver's dam, he made a promise that Frog forgot. He understood now that Brook would not keep it. The hole in the dam was frogkick small, but it was enough for Brook to slip through. Brook widened the hole as he went, taking twigs and the stones with him as he rushed faster and faster to the other side. The next day Frog waited by the shores of River. He heard no singing. He missed it. The day after was the same. He missed Brook's singing even more. All Frog heard was the rush and roar of the falls where River tumbled at the salty water below. On the third day, Frog reached the ocean and looked and listened for his best friend Brook. But Brook was gone forever. His singing mingled in the waves and he was lost. Frog felt very lonely, then. From that day, Frog pretends he has no words.

When the waters sing to him, he flicks his tongue and answers, Rivet.

. . .

It is a measure of the need for participation in stories that I thought "Brook" was about Friendship – which it is, of course. Yet rereading Mourning Dove's novel, *Cogewea*, I have wondered if the story of Brook is not also about something else.

Christine Quintasket, later Morning Dove and later still Mourning Dove, in one of those reclamatory shifts of identity and reality, is a fascinating figure. As the first Native American woman to publish a novel in English, she presents an unheard-unsaid lesson about that gap between the preserver and that which is to be preserved, as well as about the gap between the mixture of her bloods, the process of reclamation, and the gap between editor and storywriter, especially the editor who wants her to highlight Indian themes and concerns when she wishes primarily to highlight her abilities to write a story. She is not the first Indian – nor by any means the last – whose literary career blossoms and then fades, whatever the reasons.[1]

She was, fortunately for us, a strong woman. Born in a canoe while her mother was crossing the Kootenay River, she herself liked to say that her "tomboyish" behavior was due to the fact that her first garment – lent to her mother, Lucy – was a man's shirt. Her parents were both self-sacrificing and her mother was generous to an extreme, sharing their food with neighbors even when they had little, or going hungry herself so that her children had something to eat. In addition, Mourning Dove grew up with stories about such things as her great-grandmother fighting a Grizzly Bear for the rights to a berry patch, using only a pointed stick which she jammed in the Grizzly's mouth each time he charged. After several hours the bear departed broken, leaving the grandmother, who sustained only a few scratches, the patch of berries.

Indeed, the young Christine's encounter with mission education resembles the storied tenacity of her grandmother. Her first encounter with it left her traumatized and ill, results attributed to her arriving at the Goodwin Mission School where the other girls were allowed to speak only English (and were severely punished for breaking this rule) while she was able to speak only Salish, and when she uttered the only words she knew, the nuns punished her by increasing the isolation she already felt by locking her in a dark closet. Certainly enough to set you back, to turn you forever away from the berry patch of education – but within a few years, Christine was back at Goodwin and then on to Fort Shaw Indian School after that. Even after she had drafted her novel, *Cogewea*, she enrolled in a Calgary business college in an attempt to improve both her English grammar – which never was good – and her typing.

Her storytelling abilities, as well as her interest and need to tell them, perhaps, came from an old woman Christine found wandering in the snowy woods one day. The old woman, mortally stricken because there was no one in the world who needed her, told Christine to leave her alone. Christine ran home to tell her mother about the strange woman and her mother immediately went out, found the woman, and invited her into their home to stay as long as she liked. The family adopted this woman, Teequalt, as a grandmother, and it is presumed to be Teequalt, a marvelous storyteller, who gave the future novelist her moral, spiritual, and traditional training – and it must be said in a very Indian way, through stories. Teequalt is also presumed to be the real-life model for the sections in *Cogewea* – some of the most pleasurable and orally linked sections in the entire novel – where the grandmother, Stemteema, instructs her halfblood granddaughter and tries to help her envision the future, especially the unhappy future that will come at the hands of her suitor, the dishonest and duplicitous Easterner, Densmore who, unlike Mourning Dove's first husband, Hector McLeod, is neither violent nor abusive.

Out of this background we get Mourning Dove, writing in the evenings after a hard day's labor in migrant fields, intent on correcting the image of the stoical Indian found in so much Western writing as well as bridging the gap between the two races, trying to create a voice to bring the two races closer together in understanding. Sometime around 1915, after completing her novel, she met Lucullus V. McWhorter, and by 1916, they had begun the collaboration that would result in the publication of *Cogewea* in 1927. McWhorter was a crusader on the side of Indians, especially the Nez Perce, and he saw in Mourning Dove a hope for her to become the voice of her people and her writing the vehicle for vastly increasing white understanding of them while preserving Salishan feelings, attitudes, and ideas. He worked tirelessly to help his friend Mourning Dove make *Cogewea* into a "publishable" book – a dangerous effort as any teacher of creative writing knows.

Cogewea remains an important novel – historically as well as aesthetically – and, as Louis Owens suggests, complicated by the tension between editor McWhorter's voice and Mourning Dove's voice. In addition to being a novel worth reading for a variety of reasons (cultural, historical, feminist, linguistic appropriation, etc.), it also serves up a twofold lesson which resembles the double meaning of grandfather's story about Brook. Whereas it is true that Brook is not a very honorable friend to his helper Frog, it is also true that the story is both about voice – how it may be lost in the ocean-wide waters of the mainstream, as well as about how you can kill the talents of someone you admire by helping him beyond his (or your own) nature.

When Hum-Ishu-Ma (the aural-Indian spelling of Mourning Dove, also used by Christine) began the collaboration – and collaboration is the most precise term, connoting a relationship a full step beyond the platinum shred of editorial – she entered it from a position of weakness in English grammar and tense which, as she herself suggests in the notes Jay Miller has put together as *Mourning Dove: A Salishan Autobiography,* was always bad. We might also assume that as it is not her people's way to press themselves forward into notoriety and as it is her people's way, in addition to this sort of inherent shyness or devaluation of public notice, to tell things indirectly and roundabout, she began with an inward determination or willingness to cooperate with her "editor." I will presume to suggest that she withheld speaking out objections to McWhorter's changes to her manuscript, hinting at them perhaps, or shaping them into the sound of a question, so that the perception of McWhorter as a kind of editorial freight train on open track is modified by the knowledge that it was Hum-Ishu-Ma who set the switches and cleared the track in the first place. I imagine that she may have gone so far as to tell herself that the main thing was to get her novel published because her intention of bringing about understanding between the races as well as representing the mix-blood living in the midst of a dominant culture was the important thing. What came after publication was what mattered (and perhaps, like Henry James, when the New York Edition of her work was undertaken, she would have the power and stature in the publishing world to correct editorial mistakes and enter the changes she desired). It was the beginning of a career that would serve her people. That's what mattered.

As the changes find their way into the manuscript, a tension grows between her private wishes and her public acquiescence or assent. The tension is fed by the conflict between the apparent unimportance of individual changes – this paragraph or that page – and the cumulative effect of them. Indeed, the tension resembles the living tension of the mix-blood existing between cultures, a dialogic tension which unrecognized can make one insipid or difficult (or in some cases, both). Hum-Ishu-Ma never was insipid.

It may also be a tension between time and Time. The novel as we have it establishes a temporal structure in its opening which is representationally realistic, using metaphorical language and setting the individual against her own past (or individuals against their common past):

> It was sunset on the river Pend d'Oreille. The last rays of the day-God, gliding through the tangled vines of the great porch of the homestead of the Horseshoe Brand Ranch, fell upon a face of rare type. The features were rather prominent and well defined. The rich olive complexion, the grave, pensive countenance, proclaimed a proud descent from the only true American – the Indian. Of mixed blood was Cogewea; a "breed"! – the socially ostracized of two races. Her eyes of the deepest jet, sparkled, when under excitement, like the ruby's fire. Hair of the same hue was as lustrous as the raven's

wing, falling when loose, in great billowy folds, envelop-
ing her entire form. Her voice was low and musical,
with a laugh to madden the gods.

Cogewea's mother had died when she was but a small
child, and her father, Bertram McDonnald, had followed the gold rush to Alaska. . . .

Such was Cogewea: "Chipmunk" of the Okanagans;
the "breed" girl with the hypnotic eyes, who stood
dreaming on the vine-clad porch of the "H-B" Ranch,
the home of her oldest sister, Julia Carter. (Mourning
Dove 1981, 15–16)

This is followed with dream-like questions reminiscent of
the dream and prophecy of the opening of *Life of Black
Hawk*. These questions express both Cogewea's and the implied author's purpose and pain – "Would it [the future],
through her, illuminate the pathway of others?", and "where
was there any place for the despised breed!"(17) – and give
added value to Cogewea's character in statements such as
"false modesty – the subterfuge of the weak – had no part in
her make-up"(18). Then the chapter comes to a close with
John Carter, her father-like brother-in-law, and his affection
for Cogewea.

Chapter 1, then, establishes a realistic time – Cogewea in
the narrative past – which is chronological and forward-
moving and then sets this time in relation to the past perfect
time – Cogewea's Indian past. This relation of times produces the relationships of meaning: Cogewea to place and
the meaning of "half-breed" or outcast (nonmainstream);
Cogewea to the falsely modest, to the weak people who use
both language and gesture to lie, which Indians do not do;[2]
and Cogewea to the life which is disappearing around her.

Then something odd happens – odd, at least, if we assume that in adopting the language and temporal forms or structures of the realistic novel, the writer was partly aware of what she was doing. Chapter 2 opens, "It was the first of June, and the great horse round-up was under way," repeating the tone and pattern of the opening of chapter 1. The chronology of the story begins again, and this time what could have been used (and even left alone, unused, would function implicitly) as a broader canvas-like background, that of History, gets mixed in: "Since the opening of the Flathead Reservation to settlers. . . . Even the buffaloes . . . were . . . disposed of to the Canadian Government" (Mourning Dove 1981, 20).

Perhaps this seems a small point, but as the reader reads on, the History lessons occur more often, and he or she begins to get an uncomfortable feeling.[3] Besides these lessons, another cause for discomfort is that the language is not always the metaphorical language of the realistic novel (her chosen form) in which the implied author may be discovered in her "as ifs," her narrative intrusions and comments, her selectivity of scene and detail and result, or her "voice." Rather than depend on metaphors – the blue eyes of Cogewea's sister – to give meaning to a fairly clean and elegant prose, a heavy hand has entered the production of this novel to add adjectives and adverbs, to pile them on like the worst of cheap romantic novels. Indeed, there are times when we cannot escape these adjectives and adverbs, which are a form of authorial intrusion in novels that tends to alienate the participatory reader, makes him feel tyrannized, makes him feel he is being told too much what to think and feel, makes him feel that the writer is not sending pictures to his mind with words, letting him imagine even more than he tells him.[4]

Consider this paragraph:

> The sun dipped lower, as Cogewea, gazing out over the undulating hills to the west, dreamed on. What had the future in store for her? What would it bring? Would it, through her, illuminate the pathways of others? Could she fill any sphere of usefulness; or would she, like the race whose hue she had inherited, be brushed aside, crushed and defeated by the cold dictates of the "superior" earth-lords? She had struggled hard to equip herself for a useful career, but seemingly there was but one trail for her – that of mediocrity and obscurity. Regarded with suspicion by the Indian; shunned by the Caucasian; where was there any place for the despised breed! (Mourning Dove 1981, 17)

"Undulating" does not seem out of place in this realistic storytelling, but the lengthy rhetorical questioning along with Cogewea's longing for a "useful career" without which she is condemned to "mediocrity and obscurity" seem peculiarly weak, romanticized, and too pragmatic for the author of the later collection, *Coyote Stories*.

If one wanted to claim that in her appropriation of English, Mourning Dove did not understand the use of metaphors, of phrases like "as if," then I refer him to this sample paragraph from *Coyote Stories:* "Owl-woman believed those sly words. She danced harder and harder, until she staggered. Then, as if in play, Coyote shoved her, and she fell. Coyote laughed, and Owl-woman laughed, and she got up and danced again. Coyote danced beside her. And when she got close to the fire he shoved her right into the flames" (Mourning Dove 1990, 58). Not only does Mourning Dove seem to understand the subtleties of storytelling, the rhythm of her sentences, here, is so different from the rhythms of *Cogewea* as to seem written by two completely different people. This could be the result of *Cogewea* and *Coyote Stories* having two different editors, Lucullus McWhorter and Heister Dean Guie (even though McWhorter did stay involved with *Coyote Stories,* it was mainly as mediator between Guie and Hum-Ishu-Ma). But then we would have to say that the difference is the product of the editors, virtually eliminating the intentions and habits of the author herself – something that seems doubtful given the abilities represented by sections like the Stemteema passages in *Cogewea* or by most all of *Coyote Stories.* Even to plead innocence for Mourning Dove seems disingenuous. She – like so many Native writers after her – incorporates her own aesthetic awareness in the self-conscious act of the heroine's writing (or considering writing) a book, an incorporation which seems very Indian and very oral simultaneously, coming out of the tradition of oral tales having in them their own aesthetic, their own awareness of being told, of the relationships and connections, and of their audience's context, condition, and response. The fact that Cogewea is "contemplating the possibilities of becoming an authoress, of writing a book" (33) suggests at least an equal contemplation on the part of the author herself and thus innocence is not an adequate plea.

Some of the complex, disparate sense within *Cogewea* could also be attributed to learning as well as to the transition from oral tale to written, realistic storytelling, which *Cogewea* in some measure represents. Oral storytelling allows for digression. It allows for representation of dialect. And it allows for entertaining intrusions by the implied author-teller. Certainly, we have in Mourning Dove's novel the representation of dialect: "'Yo' hatched a truth if never afore,' replied his companion. 'Th' only time I ever chawed gravel was from th' back of that there tornado. I must a went purty high, up where 'stronomers say th' air is too light to breathe, 'cause I didn't find no breath for quite a spell after navigatin' back to earth. No! I ain't hankerin' for Jim's money to again tackle that there dose of animated pizen'" (Mourning Dove 1981, 72–73). This use of dialect – for humor and embellishment, here – elsewhere becomes tiring, at least until one becomes used to it and stops reading "th'" and automatically substitutes "the," until one stops letting the writer editor intrude on his aural imagination to such an extent that the characters are reduced to sentimentalized types. Again, none of this sentimentalized, overromanticized, heavy-handed dialogue occurs in *Coyote Stories.*

It is possible to claim that Mourning Dove learned a great deal in the interim between the 1916 completion of *Cogewea* and its publication in 1927 and that as she collected her folkloric tales of the great trickster Coyote, she applied this storytelling knowledge to the unreliable tellings by the elders she sought to record.[5] Yet there is so much that is not Indian in *Cogewea,* so much that departs from the thousands of years of oral storytelling tradition and character, that it is equally possible to see the determined hand of her friend and editor, Lucullus McWhorter, as the cause of the difference between the voices of these books. He shows up over and over again in additions to paragraphs. Compare the subtle reference to the Dawes Act (48) without preaching, as subtle and sensitive a reference as that to Mary's blue eyes, to the preachy,

> . . . The girl's eyes filled with tears, as she turned away; brooding over the constantly light spoken words of the

"higher" race regarding her people of the incessant in-
sults offered the Indian women by the "gentleman"
whites. She regretted with a pang, the passing of an ep-
och, when there were no "superiors" to "guide" her simple race to a civilization so manifestly dearth of the
primitive law of respect for womanhood; substituting in
its stead a social standard permitting the grossest insult
and indignity to the weaker, with the most brazen impu-
nity. (Mourning Dove, 1981, 65)

My ear tells me that Mourning Dove may have said the first
half of the paragraph – up to "'gentleman' whites." In addition, I wonder at the incessant brooding of this dreamy but
strong woman character who not many pages before has said
it's no use "kicking" at life and who has already demonstrated a sense of mischief as well as compassion and understanding. Besides the brooding, the second half of the paragraph is the language of the sympathizer not the participant,
the person who would do good for Mourning Dove. This
brings forth the same inconsistent character who in one
chapter says to her white suitor, Densmore,

"What has our race gained by contact with yours? When
have you considered our rights – our ideals? When have
you not flaunted your higher standards – your superi-
ority? Under the sheep-cloak of philanthropy and be-
nevolent intentions, you have despoiled us as a nation,
dispossessed us of our country, and, dethroning our
manhood and womanhood, entailed on our youth the
cursed taint of an hitherto unheard of blood-pollution.
What has been our compensation? Not a 'measure of
wheat,' but a double measure of broken promises. . . .
when you cite an Indian war where you have not been

the flagrant agressor (sic); then I will admit the *moral* su-
periority of the Caucasian. . . . (Mourning Dove 1981,
135–36)

In the very next chapter (only four pages later), this same
character *thinks,* in the middle of a long discourse on the
thieving, whitewashing, graft-filled Indian Bureau, "it had
taken the Caucasian thousands of years to *climb* to his present state, even with the utility of the various animals suited
for domestication and so very essential to the *progress* of any
people. The Indian had had none of this *great advantage*"
(Mourning Dove 1981, 140, my emphasis). These are not the
inconsistencies that make realistic characters not seem the
foolish hobgoblins of belittled minds but rather real and like
the rest of us; these are the inconsistent attitudes of what
Grandfather called their "loving us to death." There is the
"love" or sentimentalization of Indian corruption by contact
with whites, followed by an unconscious selection of words
which no self-respecting character like Cogewea would *ever*
use, a selection which contains in it all the hidden patronizing self-aggrandizing hatred and disregard for north-
western Indian ways.

These inconsistencies which seem to express two very different voices occur over and over and over again in *Cogewea*.
People cannot speak without us being told – at length – what
their speaking means. In a chapter like that on horse-racing
(chapter 7), which simply told would cause any reader to feel
the injustice and the contrasting dignity expressed by Cogewea when she throws the prize money in the racist white
race-judge's face, this sentimentalized and romanticized
heavy-handedness releases the power of the reader's emotion like steam through a burst pipe. The opposite effect is

what was wanted, to keep the reader's anger on Cogewea's behalf pent up, boiling, and clarifying until he himself brings the feeling to its release in a silent cheer for Cogewea's dignity.

Without, I hope, belaboring the point, I am pleased to find a dignified and stoical Nu-Mi-Pu among "The Indian Dancers," and yet I cringe at the stereotype by the time his participation in the chapter is finished. Look at the language around him:

> Mark that visiting, stately Nez Perce. Although facing the sunset, decadence shows not on his sinewy form. A nephew of the immortal Chief Joseph, he was young, when, in 1877, he fought and scouted over that thousand mile trail in a mad dash for the Canadian border, a dash unprecedented for brilliancy of achievement, throughout the annals of American warfare. That warclub he so exultingly holds aloft, still retains the sanguine stains of mortal combat. His step is that of the conqueror rather than that of the vanquished and fallen. (Mourning Dove 1981, 74–75)

That "mad dash?" Grandfather as "stately"? As proud, as wise or unwise as he is or may have been, as large a figure as he is in my heart, he never was stately. Stately goes before a cigar store. The language in this passage is not the language of storytelling. It is the Latinate language of someone who has read too many bad novels trying to stuff historical event into a chapter which, told simply and elegantly in Mourning Dove's way would *express* more ceremony and history than could ever be told by these addenda of the sympathetic white. The visiting Nez Perce perhaps belongs (although I'm not entirely sure why I say this as he plays no part in it) to

Mourning Dove's story, along with a description of his figure, his proud generosity and bravery; but there is no need
for the history lesson here – even though it's a lesson which
should be learned. But editor McWhorter, who served the
Nez Perce well by recording and translating *Yellow Wolf: His
Own Story* and by researching and composing *Hear Me, My
Chiefs,* cannot help but slip a chunk of his historical knowledge into the narrative, a perfect illustration of the dangers
of stuffing history, bitter or not, into a story.

We know from Dexter Fisher that Mourning Dove "was
overwhelmed by the final product in which she realized the
full extent of McWhorter's influence," writing to McWhorter that "I felt like it was some one else's book and not mine at
all" (Mourning Dove, xv). Even though Dexter Fisher and
Louis Owens seem willing to assume it is hers – and, indeed,
she does bear the final responsibility as all writers do   I
doubt much more than half of it is. Much of what we have in
the published version of *Cogewea* is Lucullus V. McWhorter.
Compare his sentence structure, language, syntax – and
even his salt-and-pepper use of commas – in his introduction
to *Yellow Wolf* to the Latinate structures found in a good half
of *Cogewea*. This introduction opens,

> In the mellow glow of an October sunset in the year
> 1907, a strange Indian, of strikingly strong physique,
> rode into the lane leading from the highway to the au-
> thor's residence, driving before him a saddle horse
> limping from a severe wire cut. After a formal greeting,
> he pointed to the ragged wound and, in a soft, modu-
> lated tone of broken English, asked inquiringly:
> "Sick! Hoss stay here?" (McWhorter 1940, 13)

This is identical to the passages I referred to as heavy-handed intrusions, replete with adjective and adverb, and sentences completely different from anything Mourning Dove would have written. Indeed, in the introduction to *Yellow Wolf,* McWhorter later quotes this same Indian who one page earlier could not even pronounce "horse": "'This is the last night I will be with you, and I would like you to understand. I have been here with you for a few suns. I am glad we get along so well. It is the way I have been with everybody who treats me right. I like good people! I will never forget you and your family. I will remember while I live. How is your heart? What do you think about it?'" (McWhorter 1940, 14)

. . .

Eventually, we reach one of those inversions that are so extreme that they are difficult to describe without pictures and arrows. McWhorter the editor takes an Indian's oral and aural storytelling English and rewrites it, romanticizing and stereotyping in the process and stuffing in the lessons of history in passages that run counter to the temporal structure of the novel, until it is difficult to read. McWhorter the recorder then uses this same stilted prose to introduce Yellow Wolf's story which is translated for him – fortunately – by a cadre of Native speakers and includes in his Latinate introduction, among his incorrigible commas and the insulting "dialect," a paragraph of elegant speech with all the repetitions and gradual expansions of oral telling, of Saying, which is, if not identical, as beautiful as the language in which Mourning Dove records her *Coyote Stories.* Thus, where the speech in *Cogewea* resembles this oral, simple (in the sense of poetic), repetitious and expanding style, we can find Mourning Dove. The strange thing – or perhaps not so strange, since most of us fail to learn the lessons our stories would have us learn – is that the character Cogewea, once she learns that she has been completely and cruelly deceived by her suitor Densmore turns to Indian traditions as a way for her to survive. Like Cogewea, Mourning Dove, deceived in a way by her affectionate editor McWhorter about how to make a publishable novel, turns to collecting her *Coyote Stories* – a traditional act of preservation, transference, and connection – but then does the same thing all over again, letting Heister Dean Guie help her make the stories consistent (in time and tense, image, and lack of digressive, dialogic circularity), to bowdlerize them in an effort not to make them publishable but consumable, harmless tales suitable for children. Mourning Dove fought Guie over much of this; the epistolary records indicate McWhorter's role in mediating between them. But she herself contributed to the inauthenticity of the stories by removing the moral endings, wrap-up explanations, and proleptic passages – anything that suggested superstition or might draw white ridicule. She in other words removed her stories from their oral tradition and took out a good portion of what could be called Indian.

In his "Notes" that follow the Bison Book edition of *Coyote Stories,* McWhorter says,

As living oral literature, these stories have no set form. Their telling depends on narrative skill, audience, and circumstance. Among elders, they are aesthetic treasures in measured verse, yet when told to children, they are abbreviated. The merit of a story rests on the completeness and sensitive patterning of its text, texture, and context. At its fullest, a story is also localized in place and time, ending with an edict about how conditions got to be as they are now. (Mourning Dove, 1990, 231)

A lot of this is true about stories closely connected to their oral roots. The details of Frog's helping Brook to submerge his voice can change according to circumstance and audience. Indeed, you could reasonably measure the age of Grandfather's listener by the details – especially given the fact that the listener, in some fashion or other, has to participate in the telling. It's an active participation that would cause grandfather to abbreviate a story almost into nonexistence if he detected uninterest; or, were the person not listening to the unheard-unsaid aspects of the story but only writing down (or recording) the words, participating at best in an anthropological-analytical way, he might change the details altogether in a combination payback-joke. Probably, since it is being re-imagined and not simply re-called at the moment of telling, we could agree that oral stories have no set form, and that *if* they get "localized in place and time," it is because of the above circumstances and need for audience participation, the place being imagined as something the audience can make a relationship with and the time being the contemporaneous telling of a story that exists throughout and ties the teller and listener into all Time. What localization occurs, happens in and at the moment of the process. Indeed, a story that is overlocalized is a story that is replete with here-and-now details, and that kind of detail can kill off the dialogue and life of a story by dating it. It is one thing to localize a story in Pond or Stream or the ocean's waves. It is another to localize it by using a Pontiac or Cherokee or a particular brand of beer, or phonetic spellings of a dialect that is extremely limited in the scope of its region. Another way to put this is to say that an oral storyteller wants to send pictures to your mind with words, keeping the localization, the specificity of detail, more generalized to allow you to fill in from

1. William Penn (father), Los Angeles, 1934.

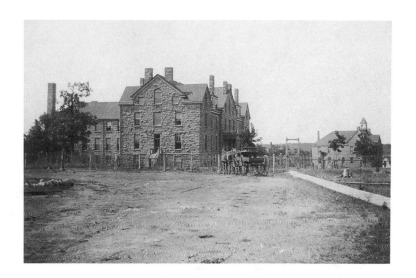

2. Top left: Nez Perce women and men on ponies, Idaho, 1870s. (Courtesy National Museum of the American Indian, Smithsonian Institution.)

3. Bottom left: Nez Perce women and men displaying blankets and quilts on porch of house, Indian Territory, 1890s. (Courtesy National Museum of the American Indian, Smithsonian Institution.)

4. Above: Osage Agency Building, Indian Territory, 1890s. (Courtesy National Museum of the American Indian, Smithsonian Institution.)

5. Above: Albert Penn (great uncle), Howard Spencer, Joe Shakahmore, Osage, Oklahoma, 1910s. (Courtesy Brooklyn Museum Archives, Culin Archival Collection, Osage photographs.)

6. Top right: Osage Trading Post, Pawhuska, Oklahoma, 1910s. (Courtesy National Museum of the American Indian, Smithsonian Institution.)

7. Bottom right: Adopted Osage baby on cradle board, Pawhuska, Oklahoma, 1910s. (Courtesy National Museum of the American Indian, Smithsonian Institution.)

8. Opposite: William Penn (grandfather) in casual dress, Anne (eldest sister), W. S. Penn (author), Clara Penn (grandmother), and Patricia (elder sister) on front porch of house, Los Angeles, ca. 1955.

9. Above: William Penn (father), Los Angeles, ca. 1940.

10. Robert Penn (uncle) in Army Air
Force uniform, Los Angeles, ca. 1940.

what you know, to participatorily complete your picture from his outlines. He does not want to paint in the entire picture (as if it could be done, anyway); you do not need to know Frog's hat size.

Mourning Dove's stories are no more localized in place than Grandfather's: the forest, the world, the river, the sky; it is not the Mississippi River, the Ardennes, or even the broad world of Keokuk. And in time, they are localized not at all – which makes McWhorter's phrase, "At their fullest," into a retrospective apology, almost, for the bowdlerization and severe modification of the stories as we have them.

Bowdlerized as the stories are, Mourning Dove still uses the language of oral tales, language which is most often described as synecdochical. Meadowlark – whose character is to be the Tattler – sings, "Two little oyster shells/Hide her in!" and the grandmother puts Chipmunk between two little oyster shells. Even though the grandmother knows Meadowlark is a gossip and a tattler, she hopes that by throwing her necklace to her and pleasing her with this present she can keep Meadowlark from telling where Chipmunk is hidden. And even though Meadowlark accepts the necklace and flies away, when Owl-woman comes along looking for Chipmunk, Meadowlark says pay me and then sings, "Two little oyster shells/Take her out!" (Mourning Dove, 1990, 54–55). The directness of language, if we can know the author from it, suggests that the relation to the Animal Spirit People is a direct one. They are involved in the world. The stories are not allegorical (or, if they are, the allegory is what the participant-listener creates, in this case about trying to change the character or nature of a tattler) in part because they are told by people who are not detached from their origins and history and recorded and retold by someone who does not feel a hint of the need to set the stories in frames of chronological times or give them extensive patterns of cause and effect, as representational realism requires. In Mourning Dove's language, here, Coyote enters no dark woods, nor does he come to himself in the middle of the journey of his life. Coyote goes to a mountain, it's a mountain; he is always true to the nature of his trickster self, true to his nature as mimic or imitator; Owl-woman is evil and Coyote tricks her into the fire and covered as she is with pitch she perishes. Perhaps one of the reasons that her language remains in the stories closer to the language of oral storytelling is that Heister Guie fought for consistency, chronological imperatives, and appeal – all resulting in structural changes – but not for a change of language. Of course, since no one to whom he hoped *Coyote Stories* would appeal would take them to be real or realistic – the way they would *Cogewea* – he didn't have to.

. . .

Lucullus McWhorter, no more than Heister Guie, was not a bad man. He was well meaning, his heart was good, and he was honored by Okanagan and Nez Perce alike. He was, however, a bit too overenthusiastic for the good of Hum-Ishu-Ma, not editing but rewriting her story, adding those passages which make us grateful he didn't write his own novels, turning dialogue into a vaudeville of dialect and patronizing insult. Bothered by the contemporaneous accusations that *Cogewea* was more McWhorter's book than hers, Mourning Dove swore she would write another novel to prove that she could write one – a novel that has not yet been found. Jay Miller seems to think this unfound novel became her autobiographical fragments, but his suggestion is unconvincing. Even if it is persuasive, the need to turn to the self, plumb it, and try to repiece it together with such frag-

mentation and lack of heart seems sad, indicative of someone caught in an almost unfathomable struggle to regain
what is forever lost. In my heart, I see her trying to write always conscious of the prose of *Cogewea,* her own oral and direct style lost to her ear by the tinny romanticizations
McWhorter forced into the last novel, her own heart dis-
couraged and confused. The one place she hoped to regain
her sense of telling a story and remember herself as an eloquent storyteller was in the act of recording and retelling the
Coyote stories told to her by the elders. But McWhorter has
killed her off as a novelist with his kindness. Like Frog
helped Brook, McWhorter helped her make her voice the
same as every other overwritten romantic novel (sort of like
creative writing programs help students mimic the most ce-
lebritized writers). Where he failed was where her voice was
the strongest, where her storytelling material was what she
most believed in – the Stemteema sections, where her grandmother tells moving stories warning Cogewea about the nature of white Easterners, stories like the one about Green
Blanket Feet which, except for a limited number of intrusions by the editor, cause the reader to feel all the injustice
and lovelessness of Green Blanket Feet's Eastern husband.
These moments – a third to half of the book – are worth the
effort of ignoring McWhorter's helping heavy hand. And
the whole – if thought about with sympathy for the diffi-
culties Mourning Dove must have faced and some of which
she overcame – reveals some of the problems for any mixblood author telling stories tied to Indian Time and oral traditions and telling them not only in English but often using
forms and structures that argue against the digressive supplementation of the oral tradition.

6

THE JACKS OF CHARYBDIS

A different lesson is offered by that other "first" in Native American literature, the first Indian to publish a novel in English, John Rollin Ridge. Where Mourning Dove wanted to be read – and thereby bridge the gap – Rollin Ridge, or Yellow Bird, wanted to be popular and mainstream. He was born into the gap between preserver and preserved, between a past that could be sentimentalized as much as the future, between the Cherokee and English, between the dream of becoming a successful writer living richly in northern California and the dream of reestablishing the importance of his father and grandfather among the Cherokee, between, I think you can say, a love for Indian things and a secret shame or even hatred for them.

Grandfather Ridge became a wealthy and successful landowner and leader of the Cherokee. After leading a volunteer band of Cherokee in Andrew Jackson's fight against "rebellious" Creek Red Sticks, he ever after went by the appellation "Major." His efforts to live like his white neighbors and to amass material wealth were not only encouraged by his wife, Susanna, but economic and social success became goals that were shared by the Major's son, John, and later by his grandson, John Rollin. Yet while emulating his neighbors, Major Ridge wrote – and the Cherokee adopted – a law that made it a capital crime for any Cherokee to treat with the federal government.

Major and Susanna Ridge believed that one of the most important forces for future success was education, and so they sent John Ridge off to the Cornwall Indian School in Massachusetts, where he was well educated and where he fell in love with Sarah Northrup, the daughter of the white principal, eventually married her, and returned to his father's estate in the Cherokee Nation, where John Rollin was born. As leaders of the Nation, both Major and John Ridge came to believe that the only way for the Cherokee to survive was by removal to Indian Territory and – in a powerful example of the gap and public-and-personal tension between Cherokee-ness (if such it may be called) and commerce or economic success – they both signed the New Echota Treaty agreeing to a settlement and exchange of land for the Cherokee removal, an act that broke the very law Major Ridge had written (he is reputed to have said upon signing, "I have signed my death warrant") (Parins, 21). This treaty – to which the "Ross faction" of Cherokee leaders strenuously objected – ended with the Trail of Tears that so many may have heard something about, on which an estimated five thousand of the people starved, or died from exposure and exhaustion (John Ross's wife, Quatie, among them).

Arriving in Indian Territory bitter and exhausted – the Ridges had preceded the forced march of the removal and established a house and a general store around which they asked the federal government to encourage new arrivals to settle – the Ross faction planned and carried out the executions of Major and John Ridge, and a cousin Elias Boudinot, as required by Cherokee law, on 22 June 1839.[1] Members of the faction tried to kill John Ridge in his house, but he refused to die easily, so they dragged him from the house into the yard where they stabbed him twenty-nine times, severed his jugular vein and then – John Ridge was still alive – walked over the body, each of them stepping on his body as he went. The twelve-year-old John Rollin Ridge watched.

Seeing his father killed and hearing right after that his

grandfather and cousin had also been killed cemented in John Rollin the desire for revenge that he would carry with him the rest of his life. That need for revenge has been well documented, however; what I wish to claim is that it also cemented an unbridgeable gap between mixblood writer and Indian background or identity. For Rollin Ridge, this event culminated a series of events (the writing of the law, the breaking of it, the punishment for breaking it, and the consequent removal and death of thousands set against the indulgent upbringing and education by his parents and grandparents and the family's economic success) that permanently created a fissure that, like the tectonic plates of the earth's surface, shifted and rubbed, shook, rattled and rolled throughout the rest of Rollin's life. While Rollin wanted to assimilate, he never quite could do it; where he wanted to be a writer – a decision and choice that seems as though it would involve the act of preserving – he wanted to be a popular writer. Coming from a background of wealth that was diminished, he wanted to reestablish his family's position in the broader world; raised by two leaders of the Cherokee, he played at reestablishing his family's leadership in the Nation. Always, however, the whirlpool slurp of Charybdis can be heard behind the events and motives of Rollin Ridge's biography as he is sucked in by the dream of making lots and lots of money – a dream that ends, in its way, by alienating him from large parts of his family, whom he fights over the reported sum of five hundred dollars. The inward tension of the assimilationist who cannot assimilate except in gold, by being rich, is powerful, and it remains, even for nonassimilationists, the danger that comes from too much desire to be accepted and rewarded by the literary mainstream. It exists in the structure as well as the expressed content of his work and offers us the picture of a writer who cannot quite handle the structures of the tale he is trying to make into a popular novel any better than he can handle the revenge-filled pride and shame he feels simultaneously for being Cherokee.

This gap, this inner tension, is already present in the nine-year-old Rollin's school work when he practices his handwriting by copying the regular, rhyming and rhetorically romantic forms of schoolbook verse in which Christ is a kind of Romantic Hero whose "story" must be told until,

> The Lamb for sinners slain;
> Redeemer, King, Creator,
> In bliss returns to reign. (Parins 1991, 24)

I can't help but wonder if Parins didn't pick this example to cite in his biography of Ridge because it encapsulates – especially at this period of the young Rollin's life, about to watch his father killed, and later killing one of the killers in a dispute over a horse – the kernels of John Rollin Ridge seeing in himself an example of the Romantic hero who is singled out by fate for special attention, a true poetic artist on a quest for the ideal which was unattainable, and a hero who reluctantly and perhaps in all humility would return to reign or help reign after his father is slain for (and by) sinners. Even if that is too extreme, it is what happens to Rollin Ridge, and it suggests, if it doesn't underscore, the conflicting ways in which he must have seen himself as well as influenced his selection of a hero for his tale, his "romance" of Joaquin Murieta, and the conflicting views of the implied author behind that novella. Like Ridge, the novel continues to exist in a kind of middle ground – and it's a middle ground that is both fun and necessary to explore.

. . .

The Life and Adventures of Joaquin Murieta, the Celebrated California Bandit opens,

> I sit down to write somewhat concerning the life and character of *Joaquin Murieta,* a man as remarkable in the annals of crime as any of the renowned robbers of the Old or New World, who have preceded him; and I do this, not for the purpose of ministering to any depraved taste for the dark and horrible in human action, but rather to contribute my mite to those materials out of which the early history of California shall one day be composed. The character of this truly wonderful man was nothing more than a natural production of the social and moral condition of the country in which he lived, acting upon certain peculiar circumstances favorable to such a result, and, consequently, his individual history is a part of the most valuable history of the state. (John Rollin Ridge, 7)

Here the prefatory material provides an all-knowing first person narrator who is sitting down to write "somewhat" of the life and adventures of a bandit he is in large part inventing. It's a first person that allows Louis Owens to assert that in appropriating the language and form of the Euramerican novel, Ridge is writing, at least in part, about himself, about his experience, about the Cherokee encounter with the several outrageous injustices invented and perpetrated by the Germans, French, and the convicts from Australia's convict settlements — the "Americans" and "Californians" — and sanctioned by the federal and state governments. As long as you know the author of this novella is Cherokee (and as Owens points out, the publisher in his preface makes sure we do), it is easy to read back and forth between the experiences of the Mexican bandit and the author.

More clearly, the narrator provides us with a metaphorical relation similar to Hawthorne's Robin as young country in "My Kinsman, Major Molineaux": this man's history represents part of the experience and history of California; the individual history has meaning in relation to the history of the state. History – the projected history of California – remains a relationship against which are set acts of injustice and honor, cruelty (Three Fingers's love of blood and Joaquin's disapproval of it) and respect (not solely bandit for bandit, conspirator for conspirator, but also for the brave honesty of some of the white men around them). But this History is not *ground* as it is in Hawthorne; the opening of *Joaquin Murieta* and the use of time is less clear, and its sometime clumsiness seems less the result of any expressed aesthetic than an indication that the writer is not in control or does not understand what he is doing. The division between broad history as ground and the chronology of the story is confused, unlike the division in Hawthorne: where the background in Hawthorne switches times at, "It was near nine o'clock of a moonlight evening . . .", in Ridge's story it seems to divide at, "It was not long after this unfortunate affair . . . (Ridge, 13).[2] Yet the division is not as certain because the next few paragraphs lead through the summary end of the year 1850, at the end of which Murieta "walked forth into the future a dark, determined criminal, and his proud nobility of soul existed only in memory" (Ridge, 14). In other words, in using the temporal structure of Western tale-telling, Ridge fails to completely appropriate it to his purpose.

Louis Owens assumes that the "Editor's Preface" to Ridge's book is a part of the text of the book in the same way that

Boccaccio's "Proem" and prefaces are part of *The Decameron*. There is little textual evidence that this is true. On the other hand, the "editor" offers his comments about the author in the third person: "The author, in presenting this book to the public, is aware that its chief merit consists in the reliability of the ground-work upon which it stands and not in the beauty of its composition" (Ridge, 4). As the third person has been used as a conventional way for an author to speak about himself, however, I agree with Owens that the "Editor's Preface" has the ring of a writer talking about himself and his intentions. But, if we assume that the "Editor's Preface" is written by Ridge himself – especially without any interior evidence of conventional play as it occurs in Boccaccio[3] – why do we not assume that the "Publisher's Preface" was not also written by Yellow Bird?

If the "Publisher's Preface" was written by Ridge, then the last paragraph may be an attempt to place the novella in the context of the development of oratory and writing: "The perusal of this work will give those who are disposed to be curious an opportunity to estimate the character of Indian talent. The aboriginal race has produced great warriors, and powerful orators, but literary men – only a few" (Ridge, 3). "A few" indeed, if *Joaquin Murieta* is the first published novella by an American Indian.

Whether the prefaces are a part of the text or not, however, when reading *The Life and Adventures of Joaquin Murieta*, even though Yellow Bird has tried to adopt the time of Western storytelling, we still recognize the artifices of the oral storyteller. The time is in large chunks which season us with the sense that all this is being told:

> As soon as the spring opened in 1852, Joaquin and his party descended from the mountains, and, by forced

marches in the night, drove some two or three hundred horses which they had collected at their winter rendezvous down through the southern portion of the State into the province of Sonora. Returning in a few weeks, they took up their head-quarters at Arroyo Cantoova . . . . (27–28)

. . .

The new year opened, the ever memorable year of 1853, and, by the middle of January, the bold and accomplished bandit was ready to enter upon a series of the bloodiest scenes that ever were enacted in the same space of time in any age or country. (109)

These are not yet the normal chronologies of realistic storytelling but are more akin to the broad sweeping seasonal times that accompany tales like Twain's "Baker's Blue-jay Yarn" or George Washington Harris's "Rare Ripe Garden Seed." These more seasonal chronologies move forwards in a line, but in broad sweeps of time, and in them we recognize some of the skill of the oral storyteller. These large chunks pause for digressions or expansions in much the same way Twain pauses, with rhetorical justifications, in *Life on the Mississippi:* "Among the many thrilling instances of the daring and recklessness of spirit which belonged to Joaquin, there is one which I do not feel at liberty to omit – especially as it comes naturally and properly in this connection," Ridge says; but this added instance of Joaquin's near foolhardiness, "I'm Joaquin! Kill me if you can!" is no more necessary here than anywhere else (Ridge, 84ff.). These digressive interruptions occur over and over again in *Joaquin Murieta,* and they are much like Twain's narrator-teller throwing in "in this place, a chapter from a book which I have been working at, by fits and starts, during the past five or six years, and may possibly finish in the course of five or six more" (Twain, 11).[4] They are there for information and pleasure. The writer is manipulating us and we allow and enjoy the manipulation.

Other digressions, in addition to information, verisimilitude, or pleasure provide humor like so many of Twain's. In one instance, Ridge presents an "auctioneer's notice": "'Honor before the 25 da of Dec I will offur to the hiest bider a brown mule ate yeer old, a gilding 16 hans hi, and a span of jacks consistin of long years and a good voyce'" (67).[5] After which notice, our storyteller notes, "I have a notion to publish the name signed to this rare advertisement, especially as the auctioneer seems to have been something of a wag as well as an ignoramus" (67).

But sometimes the humor is ironic, even bitterly so, as when Ridge gives us the Tejon Indians, putting the phrase of "naked majesty" in quotation marks in his tale to indicate that this is the phrase white Westerners use to romanticize a group of people whom Joaquin finds scattered around their chief "engaged for the most part in the very arduous task of doing nothing" (36ff.). These California Indians are not much admired by our Cherokee author. They are filled with a fever pitch of cupidity and when they resolve to manage the capture of Joaquin for the proffered reward, they resolve to do it "with great skill and caution; which last, by the way, is a quality that particularly distinguishes the California Indians, amounting to so extreme a degree that it might safely be called cowardice" (Ridge, 37). Later, in case we missed it, the narrator reiterates, when Joaquin and his party, who feel secure among "so harmless a people as the Tejons," are overpowered and "bound before they were aware of what was going on": "The Indians were in ecstasies at this almost unhoped-for success, for, had the least resistance been made, a single pistol cocked, or a knife drawn, they would have left the ground on the wings of the wind – so largely developed is the bump of caution on the head of a California Indian" (John Rollin Ridge, 38). Here we have the judgment of a Cherokee who can pass as white, who has learned many so-called white ways, and whose irony, in becoming so bitter or spiteful, seems to reflect not only on the Tejons but on the author's complexity of attitudes. True, the cupidity demonstrated by the Tejons may simply resemble the German and French and criminal Australians who stole John Rollin Ridge's mining claims and property, or even at an extreme reflect an opportunity to figure in his tale what Ridge harbors in his heart for the Ross faction responsible for his father's death. The spitefulness, however, and the willfully intolerant attitude towards the "California" Indians' ways suggest an implied author who is divided in himself, the assimilationist (which he was) criticizing the unassimilated or those who have assimilated in limited character traits like laziness and greed – the same greed exhibited by the immigrant whites with whom Ridge would assimilate and, moreover, the same greed exhibited in *Joaquin Murieta*'s purpose, which John Ridge wrote expressly to make money, to be a best-selling, popular novel.

It is a danger of mixblood identity to want to like all work by all Indians, and one could claim that the arrogant disdain for the Tejon Indians in *Murieta* is an example of Ridge avoiding the susceptibility of making decisions of liking and disliking based on race. One could lay a claim for direct and brutal honesty: laziness is laziness to Ridge, and a pacific group of food-gatherers who want money for doing very little other than stumbling across the notorious bandit and capturing him might seem lazy – especially to someone with the background of industry that Ridge had. Cowardice is cowardice, we could say, and Ridge is all the more astringent in his judgments of cowardice because he discovers them in a group of First Californians. But I think not. Given Ridge's attitudes towards emancipation and his attacks on Lincoln in the newspapers he edited, the representation of the Tejon Indians brings into focus a man who is Indian – and feels a certain pride in that – but who wants to separate himself from Indian, mostly by means of business success (and Ridge was respected by rival newspaper editors) and money. We find a man who through white injustice has learned to hate the causes of that injustice – cupidity and cowardice – and yet with the revenge he wants on the Ross faction, he seems willing to blame Indians for it, at least in this instance. He creates a nonwhite Robin Hood character who, acting unlawfully but for justifiable reasons, encounters California Indians who have or adopt or represent cupidity and cowardice and who act, at first, unjustly by our narrator's standards. But these standards conflict, and they end up acting half-justly for the wrong reasons – they notify a judge that they've captured some bandits, and the judge, who assumes the Tejon's captives are just a bunch of "greasers," sends back word to let the "greasers" – who are really Murieta and his companions – go.

The interior told-tale has an analogic relation to the seasonal, large-swathed chronology in which Murieta exists, but in relation to the narrator-implied author and by means of his spite, that analogue is ironic and he allows not just his implied author to be revealed – the implied author who is using the forms he would appropriate – but the author himself who fails to use the forms completely or well and whose desire to bridge the gap between himself and the non-Indian world by means of money is all too apparent.

Other appearances put in by Ridge occur directly, in the authorial intrusions allowed by the oral nature of Ridge's chosen vehicle, the tale. These intrusions are but thinly disguised, if they are disguised at all. Some are a claim to truth: "Their names are unknown to the writer at this time, but they can easily be ascertained should they insist upon appearing before the public" (52).[6] Others are an express evaluative judgment by the implied author: "If they had a right to purchase their lives at the price of silence, they had an equal right, and not only that, but were morally bound, to stand up to their bargain. It would be well if men were never forced into such a position, but society has no right, after it has happened, to wring from them a secret which belongs to *them* and not to the world. In such matters God is the only judge" (79–80). This latter intrusion, of course, also provides an analogue with our protagonist: he was driven to it; it was not misery made him malicious, but injustice which turned him out of the laws made by, and seemingly for, the unjust, much like Ridge's case might have been for killing one of the Ross faction before he left the Cherokee Nation and moved on to the goldfields of California.

Louis Owens calls John Rollin Ridge "shape-shifting" and goes on to say that in *Joaquin Murieta,*

> The result is a deeply encoded work filled with dialogic tension, a subversive narrative in which the surface plot rides over the subtext like a palimpsest. It is a novel that stands as a fascinating testimony to the conflicts and tensions within the mixblood author, who moves easily inside the dominant white culture but cannot forget or forgive

the denigration by that culture of his indigenous self. It is also a work that marks the thinly camouflaged beginning of a long long campaign by Native American writers to wrench a new genre – the novel – free from the hegemony of the dominant and (to Native Americans especially) destructive culture of European America. Ridge's *Joaquin Murieta* is a disguised act of appropriation, an aggressive and subversive masquerade. (Owens 1992, 32–33)

Ridge's novella does mark the published beginnings of the American Indian novel, and it is a fascinating testimony to the conflicts and tensions within the (within any) mixblood author. And Ridge does attempt to appropriate the same structures and relations of other tales of the period. In this way it is not only subversive in the way that all novels are subversive, asking readers to give up their beliefs for a limited period of time, to suspend the dominance of their willingness to disbelieve, and to ask some new questions. It is also subversive because it represents the possibility that mixblood writers can appropriate the forms and language of Western literature and to change them or use them to express what is and remains uniquely non-Western. It reminds us of the power of the word – a belief that is certainly Nez Perce, if not "Indian" – in the way that Ridge's fictional story of someone who did not exist was produced and reproduced (plagiarized) until the invented figure became real enough for some folks to propose a California State Park be named after Joaquin. It begins to illustrate kinds of language that may be used in the told-tale, some of the structures that allow for digression as well as the confusions that come from a circular way of telling (the initial confusions of chronology) being strait-jacketed into a linear form (the day to day set against the ground of history), and the need to maintain a bridge of relation between the written story and the oral tradition of Native American storytelling.

But along with the possibilities for subversions – the appropriations and refusals of American Indian novelists like Louis Owens, Gerald Vizenor, Leslie Silko, or James Welch – we see in John Rollin Ridge the dangers of appropriation or of the reasons for appropriation. Where Mourning Dove appropriated the forms of Realism and was diverted by a loving editor, John Ridge suggests the dangers of trying to assimilate to the mainstream. Given the reproductive appeal of the story of Joaquin, we can say that what was popular about the novella, what appealed to the insufficient number of readers it had, were the outlines of its plot and perhaps, ironically for an educated assimilationist, the fact that it was written by an Indian, a kind of aesthetic artifact or object that existed as a curiosity.

This, then, is what someone like Ridge, who not only desires wealth but seems to see it as bridging the gap between him and the mainstream culture around him, represents: the great suck of Charybdis, pulling Native American writers down into the depths where they are changed and then spewing them forth in a froth of publicity and notoriety as mainstream Naturalism and Realism synthesize into what may be called Environmentalism. In one of the supreme trickster ironies, Charybdis asks the mixblood writer to talk about his (or her) identity, reclaim it or reestablish it and use it to tell a story, to bridge the gap between whatever might be called "Indian" and whatever is not, and in the end, threatens to change – and all too often succeeds – the fluidity of that identity and making it known to the world as an artifact of what it must be like to be "Indian."

RESPECT FOR WENDY ROSE

I

It's possible to say that the *Odyssey* was written down after the cycle of regenerative time was broken for the writer, well after the age of which the epic tells is gone, and thus the sense of preservation embodies with it the sense of nostalgia, a sentimental longing for a golden age. The gap between the preserver and the preserved is too great to be bridged by narrative and because of the distance, the act of preservation echoes the act of the eulogizer.

A similar gap exists for the American Indian novelist and autobiographer, as well as for the novelist and biographer of American Indians, introduced artificially by European invasion and conquest. If Native Americans were going to survive as Indians, surrounded as they were with people bent on their removal and annihilation, they had to find a way to bridge this gap successfully. But in bridging the gap, they also had to find a way to maintain it and to ensure its continuation. Storytelling, for people rooted in an ancient oral tradition, seems like a natural choice and although it didn't really work for Homer (or Homer's daughter), it has so far for American Indians whose oral, storytelling traditions are not yet dead; indeed, the oral tradition seems to manage to survive, somehow, and like American Indian storytellers themselves, at times it seems to flourish in a way that makes you wonder if the oral roots of a people's storytelling descriptions of the world are not the same roots that allow the people to survive. Telling stories about how the world is requires storytellers to continuously readjust what they tell not only to their audiences but also to their circumstances or their contexts and thus it seems as though telling stories is a way, if not the way, to both bridge the gap and to maintain it. Far from being "primitive," American Indian oral traditions may be so "postmodern" that they have the opportunity to be little or only partially affected by the cartoon of modernity.

. . .

One of the causes of this gap I am trying to describe was the loss of native languages, and thus it seems predictable that one of the perceived dangers became the act of writing in English, a writing done for both Indians and non-Indians. It was not simply the English. It was also that writing seemed to threaten the orality of what was being told. The act of recording stories in words initially seemed so fixed and determined, so anthropological and artifactual, and much writing about American Indians as well as by American Indians expressed the unbridged gap of the eulogizer for the lost. Yet the oral tradition survived and, as odd as it may seem, part of its survival may be due to the fact that most of the writing by Indians was done by writers of mixed blood, someone part Indian and part white (or black), whose primary act of imagination is to imagine his or her identity as culturally Indian, but who (over time) becomes relatively comfortable adopting and using the structures and forms of traditional Western writing. What I am trying to suggest is that it is in the conflict of the Western written tradition with the Native American oral tradition that the gap was created; it's in that continued conflict that the gap is maintained; and it is because of that continuing conflict that what is surely proof of the flexible animatedness of American Indian storytelling – its ability to absorb and adapt – that mixblood writing remains postmodern. Because of the powerful oral tradition of telling the way things are, Indians who took up writing recognized that writing was not as determined as it might at first seem in its context. They could see – because of the way oral stories change – that whereas writing isn't completely fluid because words may be read over and over again, it is not fixed, either. The same words reread change their context (the book or story is finished and the whole casts a different reflection on the parts as they are reread) just as the reader-listener does (he was in the bathroom at the first reading; now he's in his office, pencil in hand), and even if the writer sets out to write the same story again, even if he copies the last story verbatim, it will be different.[1]

Rhetoric has a fluidity inherent in its use, the possibility that no matter how careful or exacting you are, someone from the audience may sneak up afterwards and say, "I agree with you. But I don't think I'd ever *say* so," when you have used an ironic point of view to carefully say the opposite (not to mention the willingness some people seem to have to hear whatever they want to hear). Knowing these things because of their respect for words and their rootedness in their oral traditions of telling or saying, when appropriating the "genres" or "modes" of the Western tradition, mixblood writers ignored their demarcations and began writing prose that was narrative, that incorporated poetic language and the line lengths of poetry, as well as playlike dialogues or stage directions, mixing genres and modes, as well as time and tense, to better bridge the gap and match up with their sense of the way things are. Perhaps – and there's no way for me to prove this – they ignored the traditional divisions because as hard as they tried to live and think and tell things in an unmixed way, it wasn't satisfying or true. Regardless, in most every case these days, this ignoring is produced by the act of reclamation, an imaginative act of identity and self that must be reenacted every time the mixblood writer sets out to tell a story, an act that always involves recognizing the gap, entering the dialogue between disagreements (European and Indian, for example), and then finding a way to bridge that gap – or express it.

In the end, then, to lose the gap, to lose the tension, to lose the enhancements, transformations, and experimentations that the oral tradition gives to the written may be to lose whatever is American Indian. It is one thing to write, and one thing to use English to write in; it seems as though for the mixblood writer it would be another thing entirely to submit to any monologue, to any totalitarianism. It is the tension between his or her cultures and their different senses of time and reality that actually presents the mixblood writer with postmodern, dialogic possibilities; it is the felt tension that produces the writer who can bridge the gap between preserver and preserved, the oral and written, the representationally realistic and the experientially true. The mixblood is the person whose comfort with English and whose desire to be, remain, or represent "Indian" – whatever that is – creates possibilities, choices of technique as well as of relations – writer to story, writer to audience or other people, writer to world.

If the dominant concept of time in North America is linear and chronological and if our idea of "progress," as Kroeber says, "destroys diverse modes of imagining" (Vizenor 1993, 35), then the diversity of imagining along with a different sense of time (and reality) are two things the mixblood storyteller offers to America and Western culture. Perhaps the unconscious or conscious sense that this loss is happening is what drives so many people towards some sort of reclamation of identity; it is only their fear or an inability to be flexibly postmodern and dialogic that sometimes makes them reclaim a monologue, making themselves and their so-called identities into artifacts, wearing the clothes, in other words, the heavy turquoise and expensive fetishes, and attending conferences to study the ways in which they should think. Certainly (at least from my point of view), the loss of diverse modes of imagining is a likely reason why people who feel trapped by the dominant, linear concept of manifestly destined time (and reality) turn to consuming those things that seem to them to transcend or at least contradict the linearity in some way – among other things, historical novels, epical and often serial stories, or novels (and cultures) that remain rooted in orality like most Native American novels.

Consume, however, is the operative action: ironically, the very people who turn so completely to consuming Native cultures in order to help themselves are the very people who threaten to love Indians to death after having made them up in all their huggable dignity, vanishing nobility, and eco-sensibility. In a double irony, the descendants of the very people who invented "Indians" in the first place, turn to consuming their own inventions, their own images, certified by the Bureau of Indian Affairs, of a "primitive" people who are nothing more than a romanticized monologue.

Gerald Vizenor quotes Umberto Eco's saying that "the American imagination demands the real thing and, to attain it, must fabricate the absolute fake" and claims that "tribal cultures, in this sense have been invented as 'absolute fakes'" (Vizenor 1993, 5). It is this fakery – not a Coyote tricksterism, but absolute fakery – that mixblood writers have to avoid. One way to do this is suggested by Lester A. Standiford, who insists in *Other Destinies* that American Indian writers must repudiate the "American Dream," claiming that, "because they hold fast to the traditional belief in the very real power of the word; and because they build on the influence of the oral literary tradition, with its symbolic density and intricate patterns of repetition, contemporary poetry and fiction by Indian Americans distinguishes itself from the so-called 'mainstream'" (Owens 1992, 22). Some does, but some doesn't. Some recent writing by American Indians doesn't build on or even seem to understand oral traditions. Some of these writers are beginning to seem to find words clever, but powerless. Further, the mainstream is not so-called; it is there. Perhaps it's an economic or commercial distinction – the large publishers in large cities like New York who spend lots of money promoting books that will sell – or a distinction of consumption and name recognition and celebritization. Either way, it is an increasingly homogenized writing as the notion of what will sell narrows. It seems to me almost as though Standiford spoke prematurely, just before the current fashion of American Indian writing. Or does he mean – and by implication, he does – that if writing is going to call itself "American Indian," it must repudiate the American Dream and continue to distinguish itself from the mainstream even as it is becoming "mainstream"? Does that mean that Scott Momaday, Leslie Silko, Louise Erdrich, and Jim Welch are not American Indian writers? Does it mean that Jim Barnes is right and that American Indian writing is writing by American Indians? And, as long as we're asking questions, what – these days – do we even mean by the "American Dream"? Whether self-made Babbitry, saxophonal hipocracy, or caricatured health care fortunes of billionairic consumption, isn't the American Dream one of those absolute fakes demanded by the American imagination that has revealed its fakery? Doesn't the dream seem emptied or more like a nightmare of the walking dead, not just to mixblood writers, but to many others who are not American Indian or even writers?

. . .

I agree with a modification of Standiford's suggestion. If the "literary mainstream" is a taleful dragon that the mixblood writer attempts to slay by repudiation, the writer will only end up bones in a treasure cave. For it is not the mainstream that is the enemy, it is its ability to transform itself at will, a transformational power provided by the i.v. of Commerce which, in terms of writers, involves the agented celebritization by large commercial publishers and the sometimes intrusive editorial help (whether, at the extremes, passively leaving untouched manuscripts that need rewriting or actively and radically changing ones that don't) they provide.

This does not mean that mixblood writers cannot hope for sympathetic editors at large publishers or for their work to become popular because the work educates or is received by an educated reading public that understands the differences as well as the similarities to whatever the public is familiar with. But it does mean that while they hope for this (*if* they do, and not everyone does), they must remember that the vampirical power of Commerce, its lifeblood, is not some editor's or agent's, it is their own desire. While it may seem that Lucullus McWhorter has cloned himself, asking the descendants of Mourning Dove to put more history or politics in or to change the length of her sentences or dull the point of her metaphors, it is not the McWhorters who must bear the blame for any perversions caused by Commerce. It is the greed, the desire of John Rollin Ridge to bridge the gap between Europe and Native America with money (and position), the greed which does not have to clone itself because it always lurks, powerful and silent in the human heart, needing to be dreamed away and ready to divert or even change our way of dreaming. The commercial power or the power of Commerce, in other words, lies in its complete absence of judgment or moral (in the sense of custom, humor, manner, courage, or mood) – a full-fledged child of the American imagination, and certainly part of its greatness – its utter willingness to fabricate fakes; the battleground against this power is in the self.

Mixblood writers who do not want to be consumed by the power have to remember why they tell stories – and a large part of that "why" has to be connection, bridging the gap that is a part of their very existence, not ego. In their attempts to be, as Lionel the elder calls getting a credit card in *Medicine River,* "a modern Indian," they must remember that their identities come from their participation in the ongoingness of Time, of the generations, and not from the here-and-nowness that makes the American Dream seem so dreamless. They must be the metaphor that they are.

II

Commercialism, imitative, derivative, reductive commercialism whose very job is to continuously recreate the absolute fake, aims to widen the gap in the metaphor until the halves seem separate and detached, or until the tension and balance between the mixture and diversity is lost. It tries to make the mixblood writer be the kind of "Indian" that the agents of Commerce can sell, and as such, tries to overwhelm his rootedness in the (or an) oral tradition. For a long time, American Indian writers have escaped the fullest pressures of this commercialism, focusing the main body of their efforts on poetry and not fiction – poetry which even in the Western tradition remains at the very least kissing cousins to orality, and which for whatever reasons seems most always to have lacked any real commercial appeal. Sure, there was William Apes, John Ridge or Mourning Dove, D'Arcy McNickle, and John Joseph Mathews. But for the most part, when the mainstream thinks of Native American imaginative writing prior to Momaday and Vizenor, it thinks of song, poetry, the translated recordings of myths and customs by (mainly) non-Indians, the places in which the "symbolic density and intricate patterns of repetition" belonged, according to the Western tradition. Recently, however, more and more Indian writers are turning to prose – perhaps stimulated by the interest in autobiography, legitimized and canonized by people such as Arnold Krupat and Brian Swann, or in narrative prose, equally legitimized by the attention given to writers like Vizenor and Momaday, and more recently, Silko or Welch, Seals, Owens, Hogan or King. Indeed, with the help of the aunts and uncles of mixblood prose, and with the latest (I count three historical moments like this one, 1820–40, 1910–30, and 1965 to the present, but there may be more) fashion of interest in all things Indian, possibly combined with or resultant from the emptying of the American Dream – which required, in some sense, Manifest Destiny and now seems lost without it – there is a real flowering of American Indian prose going on right under our noses. Not to be a stick in the mud but only a stick at the door: never has the need for caution about the dangers of the literary mainstream been greater. It seems to me that it is at the intersection of this Native narrative renaissance and the need of Commerce for a new set of fakes with which to create a new illusion of reality that the mixblood writer has to stop and long enough consider the dangers to let them pass.

. . .

The warnings about commercialism and fakery occur repeatedly in recent mixblood novels. Some warn that Nature gets eulogized or sentimentalized, reinvented as an idea that separates human beings from the realities of nature and is then repeated or imitatively propagated to hide that separation. This apparent Nature beneath which lurks the realities of nature itself is a Nature in which men and women are born of an idea, as Dostoevsky's underground paradoxalist says, a Nature in which everything is an "absolute fake." This fake is a commercial idea – "It's the ree-al thing," capable of being made "new" and "improved" in a trick of the carton. Nature did not – and does not still – need to be invented anymore than the tribes did except as a label that could be sold, a kind of conceptual packaging that is intentionally fake, a fake in which the truth is killed off by the wordies, sometimes with a quick hit and sometimes with a slow gradual death. The wordies of commercialism have even gone so far as to make their advertising fakes into fake narratives in which man meets woman over crystallized coffee gunk and their completely empty life unfolds together. The wordies of American Indian tribes have made their livings off of the absolute fake of what Black Elk is supposed to have spoken, and now the grandchildren of wordies are turning what Black Elk was supposed to have spoken into quick (and expensive) courses in spirituality and romanticism. The latter is destructive to American Indians and can result in what Vizenor has called the "aesthetics" of claiming to be Native American – a black woman writer who has used up the artifacts of being black and a woman who now decides to claim she is part Indian too, even though she has no relation to being Indian, to growing up Indian. It is like dressing up as an Indian – much like my claiming to be part black would be an aesthetic claim. I have no experience of being black. Both, the commercial and the romantic-anthropological-aesthetic, are destructive to the imagination and both are becoming interrelated, interchangeable, one substituting easily in the region of lost imaginations for the other.

. . .

Other mixblood novels personify machines, recognizing that most people in a mechanical age have come not only to depend on machines but to befriend them, even submit to them. The invented fakes of Indians are superstitious; but don't other people pat the dashboards of their cars, tell them they're good cars in an attempt to coax another willing month or year out of them and hoping that by making them feel good, giving their cars high self-esteemery, they won't perversely decide to break down in the middle of nowhere in a blizzardy whiteout? Don't people identify themselves with the engorged size of their hard drives?

In one of my favorite sections from Vizenor's *Dead Voices,* we get a humored warning about machines and our willingness to submit to them in the character of Split Thumbs, who creates his own stories in the city:

> He was a crossblood elder from the reservation who came to town as a refrigerator repairman and founded the Harmless Abusement and Appliance Bondage Center.
>
> "Machines are no friend of man, woman, or beast, and sometimes they want to rule our worlds," said Split Thumbs. He bought cable television time in the morn-

ing to remind the audience that petulant machines and rude appliances, toasters that burn the toast, automobiles that hesitate in traffic, automatic washers that overflow and spread soap on the floor, refrigerators that freeze the milk, hazy television sets, and automatic coffee makers that start in the middle of the night can be disciplined and trained to mind their owners. "Most people think nothing of spending hundreds of dollars to train their dogs, when machines are what need training. . . ."

"Abusement Center, you're on the air," said Thumbs.

"Yes, listen, I live in a condominium and my toaster refused to hold the bread down this morning, and all I want is one simple slice of toast, is that too much to ask from my toaster?"

"Don't let that toaster join the other machines that want to disrupt your lives . . . shut the kitchen door, pull the electrical cord out of the wall, and then take the cord in your hand like this," he said and demonstrated on television. "Then turn the cord, be calm now, you are in complete control of your toaster, around your hand once, the way street fighters wrap their chains around their fists, and then raise the toaster from the counter, never mind the crumbs, you can clean that up later, and beat the toaster on the floor until you feel better."

Thumbs told the man to "pull the cord from the toaster, throw it in the trash, and mount the battered toaster somewhere in the house as a reminder to the other machines that you have the power, and then, without delay, this very afternoon, purchase a new toaster at a discount, and here are the list of discount centers.

"So much for abusement this morning, our time has run out," he told the television audience. "Remember, learn to abuse your machines and not your families, take charge of the machines, dominate machines." (Vizenor 1993, 127–30)

This same Coyote-subversion or spirit grants Jim Joseph our approval as he shoots up the Caterpillars cutting a gash through his world in Owens's *Wolfsong;* yet it's also a personalizing spirit, a human spirit that invests the world (mechanical or not) with life, animates it, breathes into it, a spirit that acts upon things and perceives its own acting, rather than letting itself being acted upon, and gives us characters like Philbert who, in Seals's *Pow-Wow Highway,* has a special understanding with his car, his noble steed, "Protector." As Tom Joseph asks in *Wolfsong,* "How could you separate the spirit from life and call it religion?" (Owens, 51). The mixblood storyteller obsessively refuses to separate the spirit from life and sees the source of the spirit not in things but in selves; machines are alive in that we use them, and they become deadly when we start to let them use us or to control our way of thinking.

If machines need to be abused in an effort to let the mechanical monologue run itself to ground, so do the restrictions on the imagination that get valorized by terms such as realism, not only in the structural senses such as time in conflict with Time (Silko's *Ceremony* or Momaday's *Ancient Child*) or tense shifting its way into an accommodation of this conflict, but also in ideas of actuality and the reductions of detail. Ishmael Reed's narrator in *Yellow Back Radio Broke Down* says to Bo Schmo, the literary critic, So what if I don't have all my bubblegum machines in place? a question that should have

struck fear into the hearts and dreams of all those who believe in a time without Einsteinian relativity and a critical reality that gets taken as actual (or meaningful). Bo Schmo,
who at the time was believed to "represent" the enormous
critic Irving Howe, reappears as critics like J. Hillis Miller,
who writes that you would think "that by now the reality
principle, growing more dominant as civilization grows,
would have made storytelling obsolete" (Hillis Miller, 68).
Perhaps I do not understand Miller properly. But a mixblood writer presses his lips together in a dark skepticism the
minute anyone starts talking about "civilization" growing.
Ninety million people killed. Sure, some by "accident," but
that still leaves millions who were shoved into forced labor
and starved or beaten to death and millions more who were
moved into the ghetto and then shot – men, women, and
babies – with the same conviction and determination and
plan that the Germans had with the Jews, and so when Jim-
mie Durham writes, "Here is the real truth: I absolutely hate
this country. Not just the government, but the culture, the
group of people called Americans. The country. I hate the
country. I HATE AMERICA" (Swann & Krupat, eds., 163) he,
in part, means the culture that can hide behind words like
"civilization" from the past that has created the potential of
its future – in which it seems to need the absolute fake of the
American Indian. Whatever this "reality principle" is, the
mixblood immediately asks, "Whose reality?" Is it the same
"reality" that in its dominance seems to be monologic and to-
talitarian? If civilization is growing and the reality principle
is becoming more dominant, and if it is true that those things
would make storytelling obsolete, then why is there this
jumbo-sized need in America – witness the phenomenal pro-
liferation of college creative writing programs over the past

twenty-five years – in the face of this reality for people to try to tell stories?

No one knows more than a mixblood storyteller how easily, whether in a high school chemistry lab or in a history textbook, reality may be invented and faked. One of the ways it is being faked is with what I call here-and-now details in a period of Literary Environmentalism, where homogenized characters become case studies replete with sociological or anthropological details. Whether it is putting more "Hopi" into your novel or "placing" your characters or whatever enhancement of realism is called for, these details are the details of the nightly news, details that are aimed at tricking us into believing that the story of civilization itself has changed and not just its context, with the underlying implication that a change in the story would be a new and improvement. At the extreme, these details are detritus, things (not images but signs) of the here and now that people want to take as important because they don't want to admit how many of them and how much of our reality could be thrown away as we remain doggedly unprepared for the long littleness of life.

At the less-than-extreme, these are details of realism and fact (realism in novels, fact in autobiography) which may mean nothing but which many people seem not to know mean nothing as though they participate in an enforced thoughtlessness or amnesia. Details of fact involve the questions: did this really happen or did she really say that? Anyone who has tried to grapple with the eels of memory knows that even when he is one-hundred-percent sure that something happened or someone said that, his surety is relative to himself, the context, the *perceived* context, and that the same rememory may well transform itself if used in a different context. He is pretty sure something happened in a certain way at the moment of telling.

Whether Grandfather didn't do broccoli or Cousin Bobby hated America or anyone else actually said precisely those words is far less important than the spirit in which whatever was said was said. Details of realism may be that a character drank beer; that he drank a certain brand of beer as though the brand told us (and would tell someone one hundred years from now) something significant about his character is an attempt at the hyperrealism of the absolute fake. Some brand names have achieved the recognized status of thing-in-itself – Caterpillar, above, or Kleenex – but usually the use of brand names – for example, cars and colas, tissues and tuna – tells us less about the people in the story than the person writing the story. The same is true for things like humor: hah-hah humor is fun but far less important than the humor that is attitude; and moral: the censoriousness that people want to impose on others is less important than the customs and manners and mood of the characters. Coyote could have a rousing good sex scene with the Mallard Duck girls; the point is not how large his gigabyte is.

The storyteller still tied to his or her oral roots knows how trivial too-particular details are. He or she knows that not only does oral telling take the fluidity of teller and participatory audience into account, it thrives on it. True, oral writing is personal and particular in the sense that you tell it to an imagined audience, and were you to re-imagine the audience, the telling – the details – would have to change. Too many details burden the spirit – of the story and of the audience – and it is, in an age in which people actually can use words like the "growth of civilization" and "reality principle" without at least grinning, the spirit that so many people want to regain and that the mixblood writer wants to preserve. Fluidity preserves the spirit; too many fixed and transfixing details kill the fluidity. In terms of realism or fact, the mixblood writer has to search for that which allows *you* to imagine for yourself the scene without killing the spirit. He or she needs to try to make it as vivid as a Dream or Vision in which the fake importance of things like brand names is lost in the wash and overwhelm of meaning. It seems ironic that the spirit of oral storytelling may be what some people try to regain by means of buying the objects (or putting the objects in), when the spirit – if these people are willing to live with their own tensions – is probably there, in themselves. If they can give up their dream-catchers and Navaho blankets, their insistence on detail and fact, and look to the conflicts of their own identities – reading American Indian novels or autobiography not as a *what* for their spirit but as a *how* the writer maintains the spirit in the face of the "whatness" of the "reality principle" without stealing by consuming, they may find a connection to their own storytelling roots.

III

Perhaps it is not the details themselves, the day-to-day info-news that would have us believe that the world's story has changed enough in twenty-four hours to merit retelling. Perhaps it is not the present tense or brand-name banality of many contemporary stories, but the way these things get used as though they matter. The storyteller tied to his oral roots is tied equally to his past and his present; he knows, from the connection to the past, how trivial such details are in themselves. He draws what details he needs out of the moment – out of his imagination, out of his surroundings, out of his memory, and out of the confluence of all three, and what matters is his desire to tell the truth and not the facts. The storyteller divorced from his oral roots – divorced by the linear march of the reality principle or by commercialism – tends to forget that storytelling is a communal activity, that the "I" is a "we," an "I" merged and merging with all the other "I's." As *Dead Voices* says: "There's a trickster in the use of words that includes the natural world, a world according to the we, and the we is our metaphor in the wanaki game" (Vizenor 1992, 39). This "we" is not the royally detached "we" of people who seek peace through a compromise with power or commerce but the "we" into which the "I" vanishes like shadows in a mirror, the trickster "we" that is the "connection to creation, the last season" (Vizenor 1992, 117). It is "the trickster crows behind the sudden laughter of the word-ies" (88), the presence that can touch their "lost memories of wild beasts" (69). It is an oral "we" of stories, an incantatory "we" of wanaki chance, of Bear-shadows in the mirror. It is the crossblood voice in which stories are the blood and the food and which says "we must go on."

We must go on. The writer-recorder-teller of stories who is connected to this "we-ness" could be happy being anonymous or at least content to take his place in what appears to be shyness and admiration beside all the other "we's" who've told or will tell stories. What matters to him or her is the storied connection of himself to listener and both of them to all other selves and listeners. This, in terms of storytelling, is partly what Elizabeth Cook-Lynn means by "self-absorption" (Swann & Krupat, 57–63). But commercialism, and perhaps Romantic Individualism, cannot use anonymity, and it has taught people to object to this anonymity as an "ideal" – by which they mean they do not want it (not that they, themselves, are without ideals). Commercialism needs to package and sell storytelling for profit, and thus it tends to package and sell writers, give them celebrity status and then maintain that status if it can – in one way, demanding books be "produced" and not written without too much time between the new book and the old book. Commerce tends to be imitative and derivative: mainstream editors (or perhaps more to the point, these days, agents) look to see what has sold and then adjust their tastes to fit; these people ask "their" writers to make similar adjustments and concessions ("Take a look at so-and-so's book to see how this *should* be done" or "How 'bout we drop the second person altogether?"). Indian-ness being popular right now, publishers and agents maintain the veneer – and it's a veneer partly based on the romanticized versions of Indians which assumes that Indians are inarticulate Tonto-types dependent on the Lone Ranger to get them through, the same veneer used with both John Rollin Ridge and Mourning Dove and the same veneer that will be used with the next generation of Indian writers – of "Indian-ness" or authenticity based on enrollment or descent and, when it suits commerce, creates the absolute fake with writers like Jamake Highwater or Forrest Carter. With Carter and Highwater, neither of them Indian but both "sold" as authentic Indians, it seems that Commerce proves that it does not want good Indian writing (and I'm not judging Carter or Highwater to be "bad") but writing that is like the writing they perceive as good, which means "salable," and which is infused with what they perceive (based on popular forces and current attitudes which remain romanticizing and anthropological) as being "truly" Indian. The writer is then dressed up to match this outward perception and – if he goes along with it, and it is most difficult not to go along for so many reasons – the writer becomes the image of himself, reproducing "new" work as quickly as possible.

   . . .

Though a painter, this is Set's problem in Momaday's *Ancient Child*. His life is cluttered, his heart is corrupted by Commerce. He fights against it (most of us do) and yet he has succumbed (as many of us could – certainly I could) to the subjugations of painting what buyers "want." His talent is becoming a means not of exchange (bridging or expressing the gap) but of making money. He paints large instead of small, colorfully instead of mutedly – after all, isn't authentic "Indian" painting colorful? His popularity brings him to stagnation. The dangers of Set's commercial popularity are laid out this way (and one cannot help but hear the shadow of himself as well as of the author):

> By the time he was thirty, Locke Setman, called Set by all who knew him, had found the truest expression of his spirit in painting. At thirty-five he had made a considerable reputation, having received several important awards and attracted the attention of critics and collectors throughout the country. It was fashionable – and expensive – to own one of his paintings. At forty, he was in the first rank of American artists, and he was in danger of losing his soul. Innumerable demands were made upon him; he came to understand that success, in terms of fame and fortune, was costly in other terms. More and more often he was asked to compromise his art or himself in one way or another, and more often than not he did so, for he was inclined to be passive and naive; it was difficult for him to say no. Those who exhibited his work . . . and who demanded its prolifera-

tion began to determine it. Set went along. He enjoyed celebrity, after all. . . . Notwithstanding, there was conviction in him, and a commitment to be his own man. And therefore he struggled. Now, at forty-four, he found himself in a difficult position. *He had compromised more than he knew. He had squandered much of his time and talent . . . he had ceased to grow in his work . . . he was obliged to do the same thing again and again. . . . Yes, he had become sick and tired.* (Momaday, 36–38)

Forty-four at this moment myself, having given up five years to agents and editors and nearly killed off my own dreaming with the fake dream of celebritization that began with a subagent (the person brought in to handle manuscripts such as mine that had lapsed for the agency from "mesmerizing" to "dusty") walking along the Connecticut shore and telling me that, if I was willing, she could make me the Native American Bret Easton Ellis. Buying *Less Than Zero* and giving away the hour needed to read it, I felt depressed and when the subagent wrote to wish me luck but she was having personal problems and leaving New York (and thus me) felt even more depressed except for the suspicion that Grandfather had taken care of me by churning the subagent's life. An other agent (never met her, or her me). Then a third agent named Susan who worked very hard to make my novel salable while I worked very hard to let her before she had her assistant (taken on, evidently, to make hits on writers who were not only not producing work fast enough but whose work was not moving) send me one of the meanest letters I've ever received with a penned note saying Susan was sorry and would be happy to recommend other agents – after her assistant had said my novel-in-progress was the worst thing since mold.

Technology can be kind, but it can also be cruel, and since I am not able to write much more than a loosely defined page by hand due to a disease inherited through my mother (is it any wonder I think of her often?), my letters are all done on computer – and thus get saved. These letters tell the story of the compromise and the re-membering that began the refusal – for no one who had done to his dreaming what I had done could claim ever to repudiate – of the American Dream:

26 Nov 90

Dear Susan,

(Gracious gratuity and blah). . . . Enclosed. Ah, enclosed. 94 pages. This hasn't been easy, though it is getting easier. I spent the summer getting back into the tone; the fall doing *too much* in the way of restructuring and moving parts around. At one point, I did so much that Jennifer gave me an angry lecture on the nature of art – she's more of a purist than I, though I'm not impure, I hope – and told me to drop *Angels* and just get on with it. Well, I won't drop *Angels;* I will get on with it once I've finished this. I believe *Angels* is good enough to withstand some changes, even some which may seem to be concessions to the reader/editor. . . .

Compare this to D'Arcy McNickle: "As he revised and edited to satisfy each potential editor, he made a virtue of necessity and richly layered his narrative closer to what he perceived to be a publishable novel" (Vizenor 1993, 91). McNickle changed a lot of it, but especially the ending, to suit the tragic vision of American Indians because that is what Commerce wanted then as well as now. As for making a virtue of "necessity," my letter, above, goes on to tell Susan that "I re-read [the 94 pages], this morning, so I could note the few changes and discovered that there are a number of them," and then goes on to list changes such as increasing the "scene," changing the opening, increasing the "logical flow," and "numerous other, smaller things." That virtue of necessity — for me, and the blame for which is mine — is also recorded in letters to Famous Writer:

26 Mar 92

Dear Mr. Writer,

. . . Ms. Editor said one of the mixed reviews of ANGELS said it wasn't Indian enough — which makes me wonder, Whose kind of Indian? Nonetheless, my sister reminded me that the original version was very Indian — in consciousness, attitude, and idea — and going back and finding that version, I . . . am sending it now. I hope you don't think ill of me: Angels went through an agent who was determined to make me into someone I don't want to be, and with tenure on the line and a family to support, I let her help me make changes I never should have allowed.

In the processes that occurred between and among these letters, I began to decide to hold my own a little more strongly, to be a little less passive and naive and to stop making fake virtues out of an even faker necessity, to re-member myself as a storyteller who needed to tell stories the way his grandfather might tell them, eventually saying to another editor,

1 Nov 92

Dear Mr. Editor,

. . . I want to thank you, even though you obviously didn't like [*Angels*] very much. I don't (and won't) think of you as "all wet"; would you settle for slightly damp?

. . . Lester Standiford, Louis Owens (have you seen

Other Destinies: Understanding the American Indian Novel?
. . .) all note the intricate repetition, the willingness to
digress, the oral nature of Indian story-telling, the apparent lack of "unity," the differences even in what
makes us laugh. Different Indians do it different ways,
but I did work hard on the structure of *Angels*. It doesn't
work for you, I guess, but [it does] for several established writers. The problem is, of course, that if it
doesn't work for you, it just plain doesn't, and even if I
put feathers on it, it wouldn't fly for you.

After five or more years of changing *Angels* to fit into the
mainstream, with the "I-told-you-so's" of my wife and sister,
the novel was published. Despite the compliments on it, despite the excellent reviews in *Publishers Weekly, Kirkus Reviews,*
and *Library Journal,* while the honor of having someone
spend time and money putting your novel into print is ac-
knowledged, *The Absence of Angels* is, as my sister said on the
phone, "stillborn."

It's there and it remains there as a shield against my dear
colleagues who value what they don't do over what I do. But
there is little pleasure in it. I don't want to talk about it or tell
stories about its conception and birth.

It remains, for me, as painful as having my gigabyte am-
putated.

It remains like a pickled embryonic lesson about Commerce and my own failing to refuse its attractions, and it reminds me that I have "squandered much of [my] . . . time
and talent."

So, it remains.

But it also remains an example of how Grandfather can
screw around with what seems to be fate – making one agent

decamp or another devolve, twisting the rope that attaches me to him and criticizing me, refusing to "do" broccoli, even though he likes it — so that, in the end, it comes out okay. Even if I'm wrong about all this, I do know how a storyteller begins with good intentions, lets greed slip into his heart, and then gradually and I hope not irrevocably makes a virtue out of necessity, and I wonder how many books by American Indians have changed their endings, their structures, their texture to fit the mainstream. I don't assume they have; I do assume that they have been asked or have asked themselves.

Sometimes the asking is direct. But sometimes it exists as indirectly as a magazine editor's gracious and intended-to-be-helpful comments or the "eclectic" literary magazine that invites submissions from "new" Native American writers with this self-generated "Advice": "Short stories stand out when dialogue, plot, character, point of view and language usage work together to create a unified whole on a significant theme, one relevant to most of our readers. We also look for writers whose works demonstrate a knowledge of grammar and how to manipulate it effectively in a story. Each story is read by an Editorial Board comprised of English professors who teach creative writing and are published authors" (Gee, 145). This is pretty conventional, Western traditional, pre-postmodern stuff, and it contains a lot of Buffalo Sputum, from plot (there goes *Almanac of the Dead* or the sprung mystery genre of *The Sharpest Sight*) to grammar (*C'est moi*, babes, he said. *Hopefully*, it's true). Apart from the ungrammatical and infelicitous "comprised of," let me throw these editors a few names: Silko, Momaday, Vizenor, Henry, Barreiro, Owens (were I to add autobiographical writing, the list would include Durham, Revard, Rose,

Barnes, Cook-Lynn and a host of others). From that "advice," I'd guess that they would all be rejected by this board of English professors (even though some are nominally American Indian), that the magazine that wants "new" Native American writers does not want any of the digressive circularity of the oral tradition but wants to cash in on the current popularity of things Indian.

IV

There is a long littleness to life. But there is also a magnificence when life is connected to all other lives and storytelling grown out of a strong oral tradition contextualizes tense, creates a transformational realism that surrounds even the limited present tense to give largeness to the littleness. From the perspective of orality, all stories – good or bad, handed down or made anew – are told after the fact, and thus they get their meaning from reflection on the past and the connection with tradition. This happened, yes, and now that I've thought about it and am saying the story to you, this is (possibly) what its having happened means. It is the reflection of the listener-reader, with the help of the reflected storyteller as well as his or her skill at recreating the story in words that gives a story its moral meaning; the sense of reflection, connection, or contextualization may only be given up at the risk of meaning. Stories worth hearing cannot deny their heritage in the oral tradition of telling and telling again – to get it right, as Grandfather says, or just to get it at all – and telling requires the freedom, the dialogic flexibility of the teller to transform the details into whatever is necessary for the story. Perhaps this seems simpleminded. But commercialism, the blood-simple of the American Dream, needs writers to focus on the minute details of the long littleness and pile the details up until an inversion causes littleness to seem big and intense. Commerce needs storytellers who are not only remote but cut off from their origins (so cut off that they may not even know they have origins), with little feeling for the implied fatefulness of time. Commerce, in other words, needs writers who may be packaged and sold and who – and this is most important – do not change: it tries to get American Indian mixblood writers to become all Indian, put more Indian into their prose and more Indian into their clothes, and then fixes them, makes them into sentimental artifacturers and eulogizers, makes them into absolute fakes and polarizes the diversity of imagination.

"The choice is between the chance of tricksters and the drone of cultural pride on the reservations," the narrator of *Dead Voices* says. The tribes are an invention of the wordies, the dead voices of the universities with their "wise doubts," and he would "rather be at war in the cities than at peace in a tame wilderness. The stories *we* remember would never survive the peace on federal reservations. Our voices died in the cold hands of the wordies, the missionaries and anthropologists" (Vizenor 1993, 136). This is Wendy Rose's struggle, in the cities, daughter of a Hopi man who writes, "I hate it when other people write about my alienation and anger. Even if it's true, I'm not proud of it. It has crippled me, made me sick, made me out of balance. It has also been the source of my poetry. . . . I work toward balance and attempt to celebrate at least as often as I moan and rage" (Swann and Krupat, 253). Wendy Rose's language is not the language of victims where the "I" matters not because of its relation to all other human beings but because of difference, because "I" was abused or "I" was addicted, and see, here are the tiny (sinful) artifacts of my psyche which has been conditioned (or even created) by the event. There are few metaphors in the language of victims, mostly bathetic judgments as easy as bumper stickers. Wendy Rose is a metaphor – if she'll forgive me and not hate me for it – alienated from the European-American mainstream by her Hopi identity and yet alienated from her Hopi identity, in part anyway, by the fact that the Hopi trace descent through the mother, and she is the daughter of a Hopi man. Despite these alienations – which she could easily preserve as artifacts if she were so inclined – out of the tension between and among she struggles to create a balance, to bridge the gap, preserving without pickling, preserving in an active, tension-filled, dialogic recreation of herself every time she begins to write or tell. It is the act of reclaiming her identity, of reestablishing who she is in relation to everything around her then and now, that keeps her in dialogue. It is the tension between her cultures and senses of things like time that actually present her with postmodern, dialogic probabilities, that makes her work, as Arnold Krupat so aptly calls it, cosmopolitan, and that keeps her from being a fake.

Ultimately, it's the act of reclamation of identity that keeps a mixblood writer because, if he or she is honest, he cannot become all one thing, one artifact, one kind of writer. She or he is a metaphor, and the oral sense of time and tense and the participation in the ongoingness of time makes the immediate here-and-nowness of the American Dream dreamless. It is the strong sense of relation to the grandfathers and grandmothers, as well as to the children and the children's children, that makes the celebritization of the literary mainstream less, if not un-, important and that gives the writer or storyteller a sense of the necessary power of the word. It is even the awareness of the constructs of narrative time that

creates the dialogue of mixblood prose as well as the underlying (or overt?) sense that a good story is told and retold,
that all stories worth hearing are versions of stories that have
been heard, that while stories come into words after the fact,
they also bring the listener-reader into being, into a maturity
where you understand that you may even alter your identification by adding an eff to your wolfish nature, but if you do
it to hide from yourself or others, to try to escape from time,
or to get something for yourself ("trade" on the beads of that
second eff), you might end up consuming yourself. That
seems to be partly the meaning of Rose's lines,

> I am building myself.
> There are many roots.
> I plant, I pick, I prune.
> I consume. (Swann and Krupat, 261)

. . .

All good stories contain in themselves something about the
act of storytelling or storywriting – which is to say that all
good stories contain within themselves their own aesthetic
and usually a discoverable awareness of this aesthetic. Sim-
ilarly, one might argue that all good Native American sto-
rytellings contain in themselves some aspect of re-membering. Even a fullblood storyteller would have to reclaim
herself from the absolute fake invented for her by the American imagination. Thus, we can say that the mixblood writer
– urban or rural – lives in metaphor with Wolf and Coyote in
the heart. She has for the most part lost her language and replaced it with English; she is part European (or Other) and
part Native American. Oftentimes, she has not grown up
with the traditions of her people but has grown up in the life
of the cities which amuses her but which also confuses her

because she continues to believe in regeneration, the earning by a just and true life the respect of people who speak after she passes on, and in the absolute value of speaking truly. Re-membering is not the action of the mixblood alone, true. It is the action of any storyteller tying herself into a tradition. But Commerce's goal is to incrementally shorten traditions — and in the American imagination and American Dream, Commerce is, if Umberto Eco is right, and has always been, if de Tocqueville was right, the European-American tradition itself.

For the mixblood to be a storyteller who is mixblood, she must keep one foot in the tradition that is not commercial, not European, not willing to fall away into artifactuality. Every time she sets out to tell a story, she has to bridge the gap, to piece herself-as-storyteller together again. Her great-grandfather is John Rollin Ridge who began the process of appropriating the language and structures of the Tale and was injured by a desire for wealth; her grandmother is Mourning Dove, who takes up the language and grammar of metaphorical realism, and who teaches her what can be done by a loving editor; her uncles are McNickle, Momaday, and Vizenor, and her cousins Silko, Owens, King, Hogan, Rose, Barnes, Revard, Durham, and a whole host of other relatives. And she always has that other side, the younger oral tradition that, as atrophied as sometimes it seems, produces Homer and all the European and Euramerican storytellers who follow. So she must recreate herself *in relation;* like Cole McCurtain in *The Sharpest Sight,* she must find her balance and her brother(s) *in herself.* Like Wendy Rose, in this process of remembering, she learns pride of ancestor and descendant and humility of herself in relation to their vastness and this humility causes her to feel, even if she would want to ignore it, the attraction and doom of celebritization. In relation, she knows the journey on this earth will end and thus she works not for her end but for those who journeyed before and those who journey after her.

She may have tried or may have a relative (and we are all relatives) who tried to take up the Euramerican Dream, and the heart-known discomfort caused by that trying places her outside the mainstream; even though in it, she may not be of it. Like Cogewea or Joaquin Murieta, Lionel or Set,[2] she has through the irony of historical circumstance developed a view of the mainstream which makes her suspicious of its glad-hand hyping and self-congratulatory giving of prizes, awards, National Endowment grants, and contracts to friends.

In *Ceremony,* Tayo tells us that "only a few people knew that the lie was destroying the white people faster than it was destroying Indian people. But the effects were hidden, evident only in the sterility of their art, which continued to feed off the vitality of other cultures, and in the dissolution of their consciousness into dead objects: the plastic and neon, the concrete and steel" (Silko 1977, 204). The "feeding," if Eco is correct, is the art of creating the absolute fake. Lester A. Standiford's repudiation of the American Dream in relation to Native writers means rejecting the valuation of the "mainstream" – in itself a subversive act when everything is connected. "Contracts" can be like treaties, and the siren song of recognition and "reputation" (which is only notoriety) is loud and powerfully seductive. The Native storyteller has to be careful that someone else (including her unbalanced self) isn't making her in order to love her to death. There is nothing implicitly wrong with being paid to tell stories – much like Lionel in *Medicine River* – but the storyteller must never forget the purpose of telling stories. As Tina

Marie Freeman-Villalobos has said about her story, "The Way It Was": it "was written for [her children] Jasmine and Adrian so they would know" (Lesley, 376). When Grandfather says he doesn't do cheese, he does not mean that he doesn't consume fistfuls of it. He means he does not participate in the illusions of participation which drive father out cheese-tasting of a Sunday afternoon. He means the "reality principle" is like the emperor's clothes and that his dreams are different, and a good day for dreaming is not to be given up easily.

EPILOGUE

Indians are popular right now. It seems as though everywhere you look you find gallery openings of Native arts and crafts, new books by and about Native or mixblood writers, people listening to Native music and song and trying to dance, movies like "Dunces with Wolves" that dress Indian women in Eastern beaded buckskin with hair by Bloomies or make Indian men into sentimentalists who shout "You are my brother!" from the ends of stories. "They" – that ubiquitous unfair pronoun of people – seem to be loving American Indian writing as never before.

> Ilpswetsichs was going about the world eating everything in his path. He ate Cedar and Pine, he ate Salmon and Bear and Elk. When Snow Bird asked Ilpswetsichs why he did this, he said to her he was hungry, and tried to eat her. His hunger is great. He would have devoured the world, except for Coyote. Coyote saw Ilpswetsichs eating. He was eating everything in his path. So he goes to Ilpswetsichs and says, "Ilpswetsichs, if you continue, you will eat the whole world up and there will be nothing." Ilpswetsichs did not care. He was so very hungry.

So Coyote thought and he thought. He made a plan. Hiding a knife between his legs he got close to the monster Ilpswetsichs and arrumph! the monster swallowed Coyote whole. Coming awake in his stomach, Coyote pulled the knife from between his legs and began to saw his way out. Ilpswetsichs roared. He made a bargain with Coyote. He would give Coyote the mountains and the high plains. Coyote was not fooled by such promises. He kept sawing and sawing. Soon, the knife cut through the monster's skin. Ilpswetsichs ran north and south, east and west, roaring with pain. Coyote kept cutting and cutting until the hole was big enough for him to escape. The monster fell dead. Where he clawed at the sky came lightning and rain. The rain made rivers for the Salmon. The lightning guided their way. Where the drops of blood had fallen on the earth rose the Nu-mi-pu, the Human Beings. They still tell stories of Coyote and Snow Bird, Badger and Frog.

The monster may be many things, part of a legendary oral past as well as part of a legendary present. If, for the moment, we understand Ilpswetsichs as the "reality principle" as well as the commercialism that closes its final chapters, we can understand the mixblood as the Human Beings who, regenerated by Coyote's trickster actions, tell and hear stories. Ironically, what mixblood storytellers may help non-Indians to do—in their language that they made Grandfather learn—is to teach them how, if not where, to pitch their tense by the three pines where origins, present, and future are *not felt but known* in the heart.

As Coyote knows, Wolf and he are brothers; he would always bring Wolf back to the world because without Wolf, who would know Coyote's difference? It seems ironic that mix-blood writers could help take away the nightmare of commercialism by teaching anyone who wanted to listen how to *tell* stories again – stories that are true or moral or just, and happy in the ways the storyteller and listener remerge with what is human and may be told, stories in which words mean something like synecdoche and gain metaphorical power from the depth of time, tense, and the variety of contexts. Mixbloods, however, en-gapped as their consciousnesses are, must be very, very careful not to let others direct the stories and make Indian up to be superficially mystical, hug-a-tree environmentalists – or any other monologue. We must keep Coyote's trickster transformations and remember that you cannot teach mysticism or dreaming, balance or harmony. You either hear Grandfather and Grandmother, see them as Mundo in *The Sharpest Sight* sees his Viejo, or you don't.

Why would American Indian storytellers want to do this?

"It's a question," Grandfather says.

8

LIVE DOUBTS AND WHIPPING CREAM

Talent is not only a means of exchange but also a burden, and whenever I decide that Mourning Dove made a mistake in working with Lucullus McWhorter, or that John Rollin Ridge's hatred for Abraham Lincoln signaled a confusion that made politics out of pie, Grandfather burdens me with a question: "What makes you so all-fired sure?"

If I try to answer him – as once I did, a half-life ago – with the tight-lipped certainty of proud and righteous youth, his face sags in an impersonation of Richard Nixon. He looks off in the distance for two minutes longer than a moment and then says something, comparing, perhaps, the life of my brain to a cauliflower.

Whatever he said would be said with the same humor that he'd used when he turned on my cousin Bobby and said "Would you shut up?" just before Bobby snapped the plastic tip off the whipped cream canister and sprayed the living room – the only room large enough for the series of card tables clothed for the Thanksgiving banquet – walls and ceiling and, if we weren't quick to duck, us, his cousins and aunts and uncles and, yes, in the irony of Bobby's pie-filled confusion, himself.

Grandmother rushed around wiping things with dishcloths, trying to calm Bobby, tell him it was an accident, that it had not been his fault, that these canisters were always exploding on folks. Bobby was unconsoled. He just sat there as calculatedly calm as when he snapped the tip with his thumb while the can pointed straight up at the ceiling. It was Bobby's generalized version of leaving loose the top of the saltshaker – as one year my brother-in-law did – and, as later when he was arrested and tried and convicted for desecrating the American flag by making it into a ribbon shirt and he chose to leave the country of his birth after he got out of jail, just that much more extreme, as every statement Bobby made.

"For god's sake," his father might say, exasperated. "It's just a shirt. Just 'cause one judge is an escapee from the social security set doesn't mean the whole country is bad."

Did to Bob. A loosened saltshaker tricked one person; Bobby's little explosions were aimed to get everyone because everyone was complicit.

He wasn't, I'd guess, particularly happy in his family life. But it was all he had. Weeks before he wore that shirt to a public rally in Napa, he walked up Berkeley's Strawberry Canyon to the top of the hills where my sister lived – a walk of eight steeply pitched miles – and sat for two hours in her living room as sullen or shy (it was sometimes hard to tell between the two) and as silent as ever he had been – as though just sitting there explained everything. Then he left.

. . .

Indeed, I hadn't thought of Bobby until recently Grandfather criticized me in such a way as to make me see the lessons not only of Rollin Ridge or Mourning Dove but also the lessons of Bobby. I have not seen my cousin since the late sixties when he showed up at Thanksgiving – the day when we celebrated Grandfather's birthday, his actual date of birth lost in the fires that destroyed the 1880 and 1890 census in Indian Territory and much modified by a seasonal and not a calendrical memory – with his head an explosion of carrot-colored Afro.

I was standing in Grandfather's living room, waiting to help set up the row of tables and chairs and turning like a mobile in the exchange between my father and his brother.

Despite the lessons he had learned about being successful in business, one of which was a trimmed appearance, father was halfheartedly defending me against the merciless teasing of his brother, who had learned the same polished lessons from the Army Air Force, for the fact that I had shown up wearing long hair and a headband. They'd been talking politics when I drove in, the brother whom the Navy refused trying to outdo his younger brother the Air Force hero in their scorch of disdain for protesters and dodgers who wore their hair so long in ignorance of their privilege and in I walk, a traveling image of that which they in their certainties both disdained. Uncle was funny and the loving competition between him and Father was sufficient to sustain this teasing and sniping at Father's inability to control his own son for a long time, a time into which he threw himself with a laugh when – in one of those instances that explode the cliché – late but better than never, in walked my cousin Bobby with his unhappy red hair and in the flare of his entrance we all heard the echo of Grandfather saying, "Would you shut up. You're always shooting your trap off." Only this time, to Uncle. I could've hugged Bobby at that moment, and I was so gleeful that I couldn't speak. All I could do was stand in front of my uncle and smile, partly because Bobby in his utter silence had learned so well what it meant to be Indian. Or so I thought.

II

Like D'Arcy McNickle or Zitkala-Ša or Mourning Dove, Bobby sought a political solution or expression for what he had learned about being Indian, except unlike any of them, he did not plant and nurture and bring to blossom a storytelling career before giving it all up in the struggle to find a way to get results or to produce change. For writing does not produce change; rarely does it get results, unless it is to connect with some poor kid who in the alienation and generally common angst of being an adolescent (a state in which commercial advertising would have us all remain, impotent, uncaring, and satisfied) and make him say, Hey, this is exactly how I feel or exactly what I think – if *think* is a word that may be applied to the mental processes of wayward adolescents. But writers don't seem to know that; or writers remain – in an image of the perpetual power of hope – unwilling to admit that. Like Coyote, they travel on and when they come to the next thing to write about, they do, and they do it with the hard work and calm, fundamental passion of a major in the Salvation Army (although the Army, in some ways, probably does more good). In a way, and also like Coyote, writers are fixer-uppers, men and women who come upon a thing that is not right and use themselves up with their attempts to make it right – often, when they do *make* something, not making it right but only (like Coyote) creating another thing that demands attention and work and change. Another thing to fix. Writing is an imaginative act sort of like homeowning, get the plumbing right and the roof will leak; the only way you go into homeowning is in ignorance, and the only reason you stay with it is that when you get right down to it, it seems better than the alternatives. Besides, the interest, like the supplies for writing, is tax deductible.

Writing out of ignorance is much to be preferred for its ease. You can say what you think because what you think is limited, at least in complexity if not in scope. You can get it all down if the "all" isn't so overwhelming that the cause seems as hopeless as solving world hunger (is there a solution?; is it to be desired?). The minute, no, the very instant before you ask those questions (or any questions, go out and get your own, if you wish), ignorance complicates itself, begins to become something less or more than ignorance – and sometimes, too, at least initially, worse.

Since the novel – and the novelist – asks questions and does not always provide answers, this initial ignorance does not prevent us from writing them. Indeed, with very little discipline outside of getting up every morning and writing something, *anything*, down, anyone can finish a first novel. The reason they don't is that they lack the self-discipline. How many times have I sat at the park and overheard parents say, "I don't think I could ever write a book. A whole book." The last time someone said this, she said it to another park parent who was writing a romance, a few hours a week, off and on, whenever. Neither of them – though they must have known as one was the wife of a colleague and I am paid as a writer-in-sometime-residence – said a thing to me, to the one person there who had not only written one whole book but five (two rather stillborn embarrassments that tempt me back to them because I know – I just *know* I can fix the fuckers; of course every time I try, I waste six months in the trying and end up fixing up the spin-off and then the spin-off of the spin-off and then . . . until I have the good sense to put rubber bands around the typescript and file it away never to be looked at again until I'm sitting around feeling empty and I think, "Hey, that wasn't so bad. A little fix here and a little change there and . . ."). The pair of women ignored me and went on talking about how to keep from saying "He said" or "She said" too often, and I begin to wonder just how many times I have written "he said" or "she said."

It's clearly something I may actually know about, so I imagine they do say something to me – after all, I'm sitting on a bench, alone in the August twilight except for cightmonth-old Willy who's nodding in his stroller (where's Rachel? Ah, there, picking wild apples and sharing them with the smaller kids who can't yet climb the tree), within the circle of their conversation if they'd just turn their heads ever so slightly. Yes, one of them – the one with hair of Irish red – asks me a question such as "How do you manage?"

"Easiest thing in the world. You just get up every morning at five-thirty and go into your study (or whatever doggy corner of life you use) and write five hundred words that try to reply adequately to the questions that come up as you wonder what comes next and in one year you have a novel."

They grin, thinking I'm kidding.

"The problem is," I say, feeling the necessity to convince them that I'm not kidding, or not entirely, "you have to care about what you write, about what you come up with – at least enough to get up the next morning at five-thirty and go down . . . and not roll over and say 'I'll sleep in today and get at it tomorrow.'"

You have to care.

Enough to get out of bed (or, in the case of some, to not go to bed) and overcome the inertial despair of shoelaces.

III

That's a problem. If you care, and you manage to complete one novel, or two – the way McNickle, Mourning Dove, and a bunch of other mixblood writers did – you grow vulnerable to the contradictions. One of these is to try to put more fact, more history, into the bucket of narrative than it can hold, somewhat like Mourning Dove did. How many recent novels take brilliant narrative structures and pack in the history of, say, the conquistadors, tangling the narrative up in names and dates and changing locations until the bottom of the bucket drops out and all that is left to admire is the brilliance of the structure like an unfinished Mayan temple? Or how many novels try to be political, so political that the narrative turns strident and not funny, snide and not witty, and in bringing criticism to bear on academics or liberals make themselves into artifacts that not only *need* those very academics or liberals to infuse significance into the book but also artifacts that are needed (which here is very close to wanted) by the people criticized in order to become the people the novel then would and can accuse of being academics or liberals – or Catholics or conservatives, or whatever worst-case political or social scummery the novelist perceives bubbling before us like the La Brea Tar Pits? The novel, the asker of questions produced by the fixer-upper of worlds, cannot hold too much in the way of politics or historical facts. When it tries, at the moments of choice, of action, of speech, of thinking, it makes the author interfere and force the free will of the narrative and the characters to follow the predestination determined for them by the "truth" of politics or history. And a novel in which the characters have no free will becomes depressing – the same way a narrative essay, if the conclusions are all foregone, can become heavy and dull as brass.

But these things with which we would dullify our stories, whether of fact or fiction, are important. There is much that needs to be not only expressed but changed, regardless of your cultural identification, but especially if the identification is Indian where you can have all the negative stereotypes and attitudes endured by blacks combined with the pervading inherent belief that things Indian are past, dead and nobly gone, and thus – unlike blacks – don't really matter. Indeed, being "Indian" is the one identification I can think of to which people say with "Oh, come on!" in their voices, "Just how Indian are you?" Does anyone say, "How much Woman are you?" or "How Black are you?" So the mix-blood is asked – or he asks himself – to make sure these important things are put forward, expressed. Eventually, this can lead to the other general contradiction of being a mix-blood novelist.

Words do not capture or contain things at all and only imperfectly present their images. All words can come close to capturing is someone's impression of a thing and his relation to it. A storywriting fixer-upper uses words to create relations between people and by extension, uses rhetoric to create a relation between his implied self, his work, and his audience. In the end, he represents (and presents through his work) an imagined relation to the cultural context in which he lives and works – but he does not present (or represent) that context. Only relation. And thus, knowing those things of fact and history are important (millions, maybe as many as ninety, Indians systematically exterminated in the Americas), the question-asking novel can ultimately become dissatisfying, inadequate (how can you say it was progress?), and after writing one or two novels – especially as he or she becomes a representative and spokesperson for his or her people – he can turn to politics or history, alone, and give up the narrative indirection that once gave him pleasure. For someone like D'Arcy McNickle, his turn to politics doesn't seem to have been an unhappy one. For Ridge, politics were a disaster. For Mourning Dove, the turn meant death. Perhaps the death had already occurred with editor Lucullus McWhorter's affectionate help. Perhaps she was sucked in by the importance of what she did and, tirelessly working for her people and for women as a substitution for the work on that novel she never wrote, eventually she went stark raving and died of madness in an asylum, at too young an age.

IV

Bobby never blossomed as a storyteller but started out in politics from the beginning. He seemed as laden as some novels, and my sister's living room as he sat in it dulled with the heavy certainty that Vietnam was wrong. To Bobby in his certainty, it seemed ironic that to prove their patriotism so many Indians would enroll themselves in the armed forces that not too long ago had bent their rifles towards their willed extermination – sort of like Jews enrolling in the German army or present-day Muslims joining the Serbs. My father told – and Bobby in his silenced, explosive Thanksgivings must have heard the telling – how he enlisted over and over again in the Navy only to have the Navy pull him back out and stick him back in the laboratory because Dad was good with test tubes and the poetics of math, a numerical language no more difficult than the grammar of Nez Perce or English itself. Bobby's father had served in the Pacific during WW II, proved himself a hero and an ace, and returned with a complex composition that, once pickled and cured, made him an ace of a high school math teacher.

Bobby's turn, along with my own, came with Vietnam. By then, the American Indian Movement was under way with plans to take over Alcatraz Island in San Francisco Bay and to occupy the village of Wounded Knee. My sister was marching against U.S. involvement in Southeast Asia, and her friends – the brothers of my own friends, who in a year or two would be replaced by my friends their little brothers – were coming home wrapped in zippered vinyl or toddling around on crutches with one pant leg bobby-pinned at the knee or drooling in veterans' hospitals where on Sundays I led them down the corridors towards the chapel until one day my man Marshall stopped and whipped out his wang and peed all over the shoes of some genteel visitors in the lobby and I just couldn't do it anymore, spend my weekends with all that walking carnage. Despite my sister's marching and Bobby's certainty and my work in the local veterans' hospital that hung like a symbol of truth just across a field and rise from the symbol of privilege where I was finishing high school, my uncle and my father – and, most important, Grandfather himself – were certainly in favor of serving the country if called. So around the time that Bobby finished up his sentence for wearing that flag and left the country – for Germany, first, as I recall, where he delivered TV sets to get back at the Germans, and then to the then USSR, and later, who knows where, picking up languages until he spoke six or seven with a fluency that none of us ever spoke Nez Perce – I took my cue from my big sister and decided that it not only was not a good day to die, it was not even a good year to do so, and I applied for a conscientious objector classification from my local draft board, without telling Father or Grandfather.

v

Two things had to happen, first. I had to drop out of ROTC, which was a great loss to me. Actually, I was kind of asked to drop out, anyway. Whereas I enjoyed the Rotsy classes – the movies, the lectures with their easy certainties, the exams to which I'd stolen the year's answers, sharing the cribs with as many of my friends as I dared, giving each one a few, but a different few, wrong answers without telling them so we wouldn't all have identical answers and identical high scores – I did not like some of the senior cadets whose only purposes in being in Rotsy were to boss new cadets around and "To let," as one smug cadet said more than once, "the niggers and rednecks do the killing," while he sat comfortably behind some desk in Saigon.

Whereas I loved parade, drilling and marching and ramming back the bolt for inspection before popping the lever with my thumb and smartly flicking my hand up and out of the chamber just before the bolt rammed closed – loved it so much that for a few brief and brassy months I was in the Honor Platoon with spats and a white helmet and shiny, patent leathers – I was forced to become aware of the fact that I was real bad at taking orders from certain guys in spit-shined shoes and, as I excelled in exams and on parade, that I was even worse at giving orders. Who was I to order around some other kid? I had not earned any coup. I was just lucky enough to have been accepted into college and playful enough to like marching around with a pinless M-1 in the hot southern California sunshine in starched khaki and green. Then there were the absurdities like polishing your brass before walking across campus in the rain to the auditorium where drill was held in inclement weather, and that same let-the-niggers-do-the-killing senior cadet who gave me demerits for not polishing my brass even though he could not tell from comparing my brass to anyone else's – he knew only because when he asked if I had, I said, "No." He objected to my answers; indeed, he took a personal interest in disliking me and became embarrassingly generous in cordially gifting me with demerits.

Now I already felt out of place at this college. It had rules such as freshmen could not have cars on campus (and everyone lived on campus). My roommate, a wooden-headed lad with hair so white even Athabascans have no word to describe it, the son of a state supreme court judge, had a special exemption, and on the nights he wasn't too inebriated on cherry or vanilla extract mixed in Cokes, he'd drive us all into Los Angeles or clear down to Tijuana where we'd sit in the Blue Note and humiliate ourselves by watching donkey acts. At one bar – not the Blue Note, but a hotel bar – a huge Indio picked me out of the crowd of college boys and befriended me, later offering to knock my roommate unconscious to get him to stop drinking before he got hurt – an offer I refused, even though it meant driving home across the southern desert slow enough to let him open his door and retch on a night before an exam in Rotsy that he failed because he did not have the mainly correct answers up his sleeve or on his palm or in his Rolex watch.

But sitting there talking quietly with that Indio in Spanish, feeling related to him, liking his solidity and seeming rootedness and lack of prejudices, I felt – and perhaps this is just romanticizing myself – that I belonged more as his friend than a friend of the friends I'd come down with. His name was Ramón, he drank at the hotel most every night after work. I ran into him maybe two or three more times before I left southern California, and it was talking to him that began the night-sweating dreams I started to have. Even though – given the privilege of being in college at all – it may seem a contradiction to the people who commit injustices everyday while sententiously talking like Bobby about justice, I began to dream of upper-middle-class boys marching side by side into the defoliage of Vietnam with the unlucky blacks and Hispanics. Los Indios were not in the dream; they were all back home, dreamily moving about the Wallowa Valley or walking among the blackjack hills of John Joseph Mathews. By the end of the first semester, I was in the dean's office where the dean – with some concern on his face and a thoroughly correct understanding of what graduating from that college could have done for me in the world's eyes – was asking me if I wouldn't have a change of heart (which was my politics) and stay, if there wasn't something he – or anyone else – could do for me and I thought, yeah, give the Valley back to the Real People and let the niggers and rednecks stay home and not die. But all I said, shyly, was "No."

VI

The other thing that happened was Wounded Knee. Oh, not the AIM takeover. Nothing as dramatic as that. I have always been too early or too late, too stupid or too cautious for drama. No, my Wounded Knee was just that, mine. Leaving southern California in December, I worked for the next ten months for Hewlett-Packard Corporation in Palo Alto, up north, as a stock clerk, inventory person, and generalist on machines like the heat sealer, where you lay out parts on perforated cardboard, punch a red button and get out of the way as the machine drops down and seals the parts to the board with hot plastic. Hewlett-Packard was a good company to work for, and in the bowels of the plant I learned a lot about race, class, and gender, but even I found working to be a lot harder than going to school then, and by the next fall, I was back in college up north where I shared an apartment beside the railroad tracks with a fellow named George Bull who claimed he was part Cherokee. Then, I didn't have the feeling that those Cherokee were the lustiest propagators in the world, worse than Old Man Coyote himself, given the number of part-Cherokee people they seem to have spawned. Besides, George may have been, and while he knew too many facts and had too much certainty about things Indian, he was a sympathetic friend and apartment mate, and he was given to doing spur-of-the-moment things like leaving a bar and going home and packing his Volkswagen van with a Corvair engine in it and leaving for Idaho and then on to the Rosebud Reservation in South Dakota. He had forty bucks, I had ten, and like a modern Indian I had gasoline credit cards. So off we went, working a few days on a farm in Idaho for money or filling up the gas tanks of strangers at filling stations, using my credit card, and taking their cash so we could eat, doing whatever it took to keep going.

George took along his local girlfriend, Martha, as far as her grandfather's in Idaho, and so for the first several days I did most of the driving, singing at the top of my lungs to songs on the radio to drown out the rocking sweating sounds of Martha and George banging away in the back of the van. We got followed by a lot of highway patrol cars and pulled over by local sheriffs ("Where you girls goin'?") until in Wapiti Wyoming I spent some of our food money on two American flags, one of which we taped to the rear window and the other of which we flew from the radio's antenna. I swear that I did it hopelessly, more as a joke or a question than anything but color me pink with laughter when it worked. It was like enlisting in America. A sheriff beside the Wyoming road (where all you see are the leftover signs bought at discount from other states that warn of bends and bumps, cattle and playing children, never seeing the cattle and never reaching anything that could be identified as a bump) saw us coming — two weirdos in an Army green van — and edged forward to pull out and follow us until he could find the energy to pull us over and then he saw that antenna flag, blinked, looked again and saw that larger flag stuck in our rear window, and

in the rearview mirror you could see his car ease back like a
cat and settle down to wait the next prey to bumble down
that rural highway forgetful of his speed as he wondered
where the hell those Children Playing were. I felt in awe of
the power of symbols; it was a bit like having polished brass
in the rain. And I learned new respect for appearances.

   . . .

It was the appearance of Wounded Knee, in a way, that got
me. A small adobe church, grayed and chipped by the questions it knows, with six or seven granite steps leading up to a
white door with the arched tan glass above the door repli-
cated in the door itself. Above that, a niche with a plaster
statue and the rolling curves of the facade above that, as
though the facade is there only for the purpose of giving that
statue a home. Beside the church, two brick and plaster pil-
lars with a metal arch on which is bolted or welded a small
cross. If you stand at the gateway and look between those pil-
lars, a white cement path leads in and splits to cradle a rectangle of unweeded sand and dirt. It's a large rectangle, a
mass grave where the bodies of men, women, and babies
were dumped like so many unused buffalo. Beyond it is a solitary oak tree pasted against a blue sky that grays at the hori-
zon with a Morse code of white clouds that teases you with
the dit-dit-dash of shade as their shadows trail across the site
in silence.

   Even George, who knew names and dates and how many
bodies were planted there, could not or would not speak.
The two of us stood at the entrance to that graveyard for a
long time. At last, George turned to wander around the
adobe chapel and the clouds began to join into a distant
storm above the yellow and orange of the sun withdrawing
from the land. I asked, then, the dead to forgive me for tak-

ing a photograph of that grave and tree and the pillar of monument beside the path, one photograph only, and for twenty-five years I've kept it on my desk in a plastic photo cube that also has one of my few pictures of Grandfather as well as a photo of an oranging sky on the top – the big sky with thunder rising to a higher place, which is how Joseph's name usually gets translated. It is not to remind me of the mass grave – they are spread all over the country and all over the world, one looking much like another in its desolation and cross, its silence and solitary marking monument. No, I keep that photo to remind me that appearances do not always hide reality and that only a diligent few can remain truly and luckily ignorant, that buried below the surface of this land is Indian and that it may be ignored but never quite forgotten. I decided then that there wasn't a politics equal to the silence of that grave and that, if ever I told stories, then what was Indian about them would be buried but present like the bones of Wounded Knee.

VII

My draft board asked me all kinds of tricky questions to which I managed trickster answers. What would I do if someone grabbed my sister and raped her right before my eyes? I did not see how this related to asking to be exempted from killing Vietnamese and second lieutenants in the steam of South Vietnam because I was not in a position in society to make propaganda films like Reagan, or buy my way into the National Guard like Quayle, or smudge my record like Clinton. I was just some poor privileged schmo who had managed finally to graduate from college and I hadn't done all that cutting of class and late-night drinking and discussing just to exchange it for the nightmare of Vietnam, even though I could foresee that like a couple of other writers who have reinvented their desks in Saigon to be foxholes in the jungle, it would one day be chic to admit that you went and fought, and even killed.

What would I do if someone tried to rape my sister?

I'd beat the living daylights out of him.

"But I'd use force," I told my draft board. "Not violence."

Raised eyebrows.

"Force to prevent, not to injure."

I think, in a way, I meant it when I said it. Heaven knows I didn't have children, then, whom I would protect with my and anyone else's life. Of course, Vietnam had little to do with protecting the life of any American: it may have had to do with opening up China, and today even Vietnam itself, to American profiteering. But it was darned hard to twist the plotline of the story around so that Lady Bird Johnson actually felt threatened.

Anyway (he said, pulling back from the politics, the truth of which anyone not on the Trilateral Commission probably can only guess at), while I waited to hear about the C.O., along came the formal invitation from Uncle Sam for me to attend a physical inspection of my person. Dress, informal. RSVP not required. See you there.

. . .

I never wanted to tell this story because the politics of it confuse me still, like pumpkin pie and ribbon shirts did Bobby. So many Indians and blacks and whites and Asian boys just like me died in Vietnam; so many Indian boys have enrolled in the military as a way off the reservation and out of poverty; so much has been said and resaid that it's like a story that won't let us know how it must be told. And now, with the opening of Vietnam to Coca-Cola, the relaxing of trade embargoes because to keep them is economically unsound, it is like a story that will never get told, really. The sadness and the terror at home and abroad is there – the sadness hangs about the memorial in Washington with the power of tears. But the reasons for that war seem as inadequate as the monument to the slaughter at Wounded Knee.

Nonetheless, this story I don't want to tell keeps asking to be let out. So:

Early on the appointed morning, I boarded a bus along with thirty or so other boys, brothers in fear and apprehension now, regardless of race, creed, and color, and was driven the predawn hour and a half down to the cold entrance to the Oakland Induction Center, a warm and cheery armory building into which we were allowed after standing around in the cold for forty-five minutes – our first encounter with how the U.S. Army valued us and our participation in this drafty ritual. Men – like the uniformed man on the bus – barked at us, trying to substitute timid obedience for coffee, as up a cold corridor we were fed until we were ordered to sit in a holding room. To look around that room, you'd begin to wonder if the country wasn't forty percent black, twenty percent Chicano, ten percent Indian and Asians, and the rest white. I had plenty of opportunity to look around as one by one boys were called to a teller's window, given papers, and sent off down the line to other rooms before a new herd reflecting similar percentages was chuted into the holding pen. Let me tell you, it felt kind of strange to be the only person sitting in that room for the five or ten minutes between the final exit of the penultimate boy and the entrance of the new crowd, and it was odd to sit there and listen to the bravado and chutzpa of the entering crowd fade like a photograph as one by one the crowd was thinned.

Finally, after the third or fourth flush of the room, I ventured to the teller's window where the head of a clerk stared down at a desk.

"Wait 'till you're called," the head said.

"I've been waiting. Over an hour."

"Not possible."

"True, though. It may not be possible, or even probable, but it's true."

"Wait 'till you're called."

I returned to a chair, picking a different one just for a change, and waited as the room filled and emptied.

I went back to the head in the window. "Yoo hoo. I'm still here."

"Wait . . ."

"Look, if you don't do something, I'm just going to leave."

The head looked up at that. It smiled. An I'm-not-going-to-Vietnam smile-but-you-are smile. "You can't."

"What do you mean, 'I can't?'"

"Just what I said. This is the Army."

"Shit on the Army two times," I said. "See you."

"Wait! Halt! Hold on. Please."

I went back to the window. I looked at him, he looked at me. We measured each other and both came up short.

"Name?"

"Yes."

He got angry. "Lookit, bud, one more joke outta you and I'll have the M.P.s in here."

"Penn," I said. I knew M.P.s. They were like those cowboys in Utah who'd shave your head for sport and a politics not quite like yours. I'd met M.P.s in ROTC, in films and real life, though which was which was sometimes hard to say.

The head dropped, searched a list, a finger came up and

flipped the pages, and it searched another list. Finally, it smiled again, "You don't exist."

Well, that got me. Just what they'd wanted all along. I'd show them I did. "I do too exist," I said.

"Not to me." Grin.

"So I can leave?"

"Nah. You go to Room 101. They'll make you a file. Bring it to me. Then wait till you're called."

Back down the corridor, tempted all the way to just walk out. The sun was high, by now, and I could hitchhike home. But I knew the Army. It hadn't changed much since 1877. Walking out now would be a lot like walking away then; I'd be characterized as a criminal, and the Army would be after me, relentless and unforgiving. The corporal in Room 101, though, had to rub it in. "Shit," he said, "I were you, I'd have just walked out."

"You'd have found me," I said.

"Maybe. Maybe not," he said. "We go through so many . . . uh . . . files these days that some get misplaced permanently."

"Too late now," I said.

"Yeah," he said, and buried beneath his voice was the feeling that it really did matter to him. "Yeah. Way too late now." Fifteen minutes later, I was back in the holding room, waiting 'till I was called once more before being sent down to the locker rooms where we stripped to our skivvies – for most the first, for me the second, humiliation – and then filed into a gymnasium where we stood with our backs to the wall and waited for the doctors to come check us out. A fat pale boy crossed his arms across his chest trying to hide his breasts while a couple of black kids talked loudly back and forth across the room, sure that somewhere they would fail this physical given, as JeRoy put it, what he'd had for breakfast.

Some of JeRoy's high mood deflated when the captain, followed by an assistant with a clipboard, passed swiftly around the room with a flashlight to check our eyes. "Hey," JeRoy called after him, "I had my fucking eyes closed, man!"

The captain didn't even blink. "Better keep 'em open in Nam," he said quietly – and it was the quiet way he said it that sobered JeRoy, as well as the rest of us.

The poor fat guy began sweating. Panting, lightly, rapidly. As we headed into the next room to sit on benches at long tables and fill out forms with the pencil stubs issued to us, I dropped back to tell him it was going to be all right. His name was Henry. He was really sweating as he squinched in beside me on a bench and where his thigh touched mine, I began to sweat as well. I don't know why, but I felt sorrier for him than all the rest of us combined. He was so afraid, so worried, that he couldn't make sense of his form, so I took his form and filled it out for him, asking him questions and deciphering his sighs and groans as yesses or nos. JeRoy, who turned to tease the kid – he was teasing us all, cheering us on as we moved down the chutes – suddenly looked pensive. "Hey, man," JeRoy said, "You okay?"

"He'll be okay," I said.

"Good," JeRoy said, and he meant it. "Good." Race didn't matter in here; class, maybe, but we, naked except for our undershorts, were all of the same class, even the snooty kid who made a point of not standing or sitting near us, who refused to look at us as though he would need a telescope to see that far beneath him. As soon as he peed all over his hand taking a urine sample, he'd be one of us – and was, suddenly apologetic and grateful for the way we overlooked his aloofness. But that came later. Right now, I was enduring the needy gratitude of this kid called Henry.

He – and JeRoy's slow friend, Lenigh – held up all of us after they gave us back our clothes and handed out bubbled booklets for the intelligence tests. None of us could leave or even stand up until everyone had finished the intelligence tests, which didn't take a whole lot of intelligence. One question, I remember, had to do with what tool you would use to turn a screw, and Henry and Lenigh seemed to struggle over the answers, chewing away the eraserless nubs of their pencils in contemplative desire.

"Shit, man," JeRoy hissed. "What the fuck if it's wrong? Do you care?" He tried to exchange his booklet for Lenigh's so he could fill in the bubbles and we could get on with the fun of our day. Lenigh resisted. He gave JeRoy a bad look. JeRoy grinned, and I saw in his grin the difference in their politics, the one wanting to prove he could do it, regardless of what and for whom, that he existed, and the other who made things as serious as they might be into something to be laughed at.

"Come on, bro'," JeRoy said. "We're gonna be here the week."

A corporal of context stepped into the room. "No cheating," he said.

It was the wrong context. "Cheating? Why the fuck would I cheat?" JeRoy said. "You gonna find out I'm too dumb to die?"

"Quiet!" the corporal ordered, drawing his voice up on a leash from deep in his diaphragm. JeRoy smiled and shook his head.

Finally, the maximum allotted time was up and although neither Lenigh nor Henry had finished answering his questions, we turned in our booklets and followed the corridor to the urine test. There my friend JeRoy filled his plastic cup with a sample that he was sure would fail, given what he had ingested that morning in the way of drugs, and then tipped some into the cups of others. Even the snooty kid, once he had washed off his hand, took some, and that made JeRoy real happy. I didn't want to disappoint JeRoy, and I accepted a centiliter or so, knowing that neither he nor I would fail, filled out my gummed name-label and handed in my cup to a private who sat there all day staring at trays of urine, and followed the blue line on the floor to the next station and next exam – none of which I would fail, although I sort of skipped right by the room in which the Army was giving out tetanus shots for free.

It was at the last line, where one by one, we met with psychiatric doctors in cheerless cubicles. JeRoy was beginning to wonder why they hadn't pulled him out of line and sent him home, given his urine sample; he remained, however, cheerful and joking. The last I saw of him was when he offered me a Marlboro – which I accepted, tucking it pencil style behind my ear until I was in the room with my doctor where we were allowed to light up. I did. I borrowed the doctor's pre-Koop lighter, held the cigarette between my dry but sticky lips, lit it, sucked on it, and then took it from my mouth with my left hand – at which point, the doctor grabbed my hand, looked at it, and asked, "What happened here?"

"Basketball," I replied. In what seemed a lifetime ago, I'd played strong-side forward for the small college in southern California and, with my usual sense of dramatic timing, being often a little early or a little late for a rebound, had jammed the fingers of my hands so often that I'd learned to shoot with plastic braces taped over two of them. All of my fingers were crooked; one, in particular, had a knuckle that looked as though it was only visiting.

"Any problems with them?"

"They lock up, sometimes. But all I do is bend 'em like this." I rolled the fingers of my left hand down with my right and flexed them. "Then they work okay."

The doctor filled out a slip. "I'm sending you down for X-rays on those hands." He handed the slip to me and directed me to the room where they'd put my hands on a plate and take pictures of what was beneath the surface.

When I asked the technician why all the fuss over basketball fingers, he replied, "You can't kill gooks if you can't pull the trigger."

My god, I thought. My heavens. My lord. My Marlboro. After all of that, the politics were in the offer and acceptance of that cigarette, the doctor's notice an accident of politics in a context I never dreamed.

It was not politics that made me reply to the young medic who took my envelope of X-rays and told me to come back tomorrow, "You're kidding."

He looked up. Once again, I found myself measuring and being measured. Once again, I found both of us coming up short. He didn't want to be where he was. I didn't want to be where he was. But he was and I, I wasn't. It'd been a long day; I'd been poked and prodded and examined; I no longer cared a raven's feather what he told me to do. My smile – I thought he must be kidding – made him angry.

"What makes you think I'm joking," he hissed. "The X-rays will be evaluated tonight. You will come back tomorrow."

I said shyly, "No."

He blew up and starting shouting that this was the U.S. Army ordering me to come back tomorrow and I had no choice and when he was done I shook my head and, feeling a good deal of compassion for his position but a intense dislike for his attitude, said, "Catch me."

I looked around for JeRoy as I left, but he was gone. I was in some other part of the armory and so I walked outside and caught a Greyhound bus out of Oakland, hitch-hiking the last leg up Route 80 to home.

VIII

To justify the ways of armies to men is not possible. Bobby was excluded from service because of his criminal record, and six months after I did not return to the Oakland Induction Center, I received an I-O or conscientious objector classification in an envelope marked by warnings of severe penalties for any other than official use. George Bull was there when I opened it, expecting the worst.

"My draft card," I said, handing it to him. In my certainty about what it would be, I had read the I-O as I-A and sank onto a kitchen chair. It was only a matter of tense before I would be called up out of the narrative past, into the future pluperfect of Vietnam.

George tried to console me. "I'll go get some wine," he said. He picked up the card. "So this is what it looks like," he mused.

I nodded. I felt deadened, everything buried, covered up, hidden.

"Hey, wait a minute," George exclaimed.

"What?"

"This isn't an A."

"No?"

"No. Jeez-us, it's an O. An O. Don't you know what that means? You got it. You don't have to go."

I took the card from him and looked at it. He was right. "Not armed, anyway," I said.

George wanted to celebrate and so did I for a minute until suddenly I felt sorry for JeRoy and Henry, Lenigh and the snooty white boy, and all my other friends at the induction center. Why me and not them? I felt almost as bad as the evening decades later when my wife and I were at dinner at a friend's and his wife said that she spit on the soldiers returning from Vietnam.

"You did what? You spit?"

"Damn right I did. It was their fault that war happened. They were criminals. As guilty as Johnson. So I spit on them." She seemed so certain.

I felt punched in the solar plexus. That could've been JeRoy she spit on. He wasn't a criminal. No, he simply didn't fail his urine test and followed the certain orders of the U.S. Government to ship out to a place called Vietnam where uncondomed capitalism told him he was dying to play dominoes and contain communism, made him into a buffalo soldier afraid of gooks who were almost Indian in their inhumanity, a boy who in his fear would kill anything that moved regardless of race, gender, class, or – perhaps not my JeRoy but someone's JeRoy – uniform, shooting second lieutenants in the back to avoid being sent out on point. Twenty years later, Coca-Cola, corporately knowing the difference between "Classic" and "New," would be poised like a battleship on the borders of the "New" Vietnam, ready to have Coke on the shelves the day after the U.S. trade embargo was lifted and few people would even pause to think of JeRoy. When the heads of the U.S. Olympic Committee showed up on camera before the Winter Olympics wearing American flag shirts, even Bobby must have wondered at his certainties. It seemed as though here was politics, here the revelation of history.

. . .

One certain good came out of my C.O. application and that was a trickster relation to the context of politics. When the lottery was put into place the very next year, I got 326, which meant virtually every other classless or déclassé kid in the country would be called up before I would. My good friend, Michael – the one most people called "Meathead" affectionately because they didn't see the pain that caused him – got 16. No longer meathead, just dead meat, at that stage of the war. Cannon fodder, skewer beef, mosquito bait. Where I was a C.O. by what I thought were political beliefs (but which were probably no greater or lesser than the domino theories of selling new Coke), Michael was a C.O. by nature; he could not hurt anything, not even the mosquito sucking his blood; he wouldn't tell you that being called Meathead hurt his feelings because he wouldn't want to hurt yours. He was so helplessly gentle that women mothered him on sight.

Michael and I shared the same draft board, and it was with my C.O. in hand that we went to visit our friends at the board and asked them to take away my C.O. and give it to Michael, a suggestion that in the way it questioned their judgments of me, amused our friends at the board no end. It was a lark to them. But we didn't give up. We went back. Michael's mother went. We went back, again. Each time, our friends pulled out Michael's file as well as my file. That I was doubly protected from jungle fever seemed sometimes to piss them off a little – oh, let's send this troublemaker and teach him the lesson of lessons – but they kept their bureaucratic cool and managed accommodating grimaces if not smiles each time Michael and I laid siege to their waiting room (one of the clerks began to look forward to our coming). Pull files, put 'em back. Pull files, have someone new examine them, put 'em back. My file. Michael's file. After three months of this, though, Michael just gave up and decided there was no use. He willed me his stereo speakers and his twelve-year-old Cadillac that took two gallons of gas just to fill the gas lines, and we went on with our daily, unimportant lives.

Nothing happened. Guys with number 18, 20, 30 got their induction notices and went down to Oakland to pass their physicals before a few weeks of basic and shipment to Southeast Asia. Now and then, friends finished tours of duty. Some even returned physically intact to see us, avoid telling stories about what they'd seen or done, and then, unable to take being back in this world, disappeared. But not a word to Michael came from our friends at the board until fourteen months later. He walked in to my apartment looking as ragged as the last buffalo (or the last buffalo hunter) and handed me the letter ordering him to report and pass his physical and head off to the beaches and rivers of South Vietnam to take back Hill Number 431. He was ready to go. We got drunk.

In the middle of being drunk, Michael said, "Wonder what took so long?" A simple question, but one which struck the heart of my ignorance sharply enough for me to remember it the following day and to ask it of a draft counselor I went to see.

Turned out there were two "drawers," an A drawer and a B drawer; the A drawer contained all the names of those who had to be called up before the national emergency of calling the B drawer. Somehow – but Michael and I had a pretty good idea how – Michael had gotten put in the B drawer for the year of his A drawer liability. Our draft board said he still had to report for his induction but – and this asked a question, too, of Bobby who thought the entire system was bad, that all judges were bad – a judge said that after a year of liability, the draft board had to put Michael into the B drawer forever. He who had stood and waited had, regardless of whether a mistake was made or not, also served.

It was pure Coyote, outrageous luck.

But Michael was not a believer in Coyote. He was sad, a little, in our celebration. "Now some other guy will have to go in my place," he said.

And he was right.

IX

Grandfather believed strongly in his sons and his grandsons serving their country because he believed that it proved that Indians were loyal and courageous and honorable. Where he came from – and where so many friends and acquaintances come from – joining the armed services could also be a ticket out of poverty or trouble, a perfectly respectable action to take. But I had ROTC to question whether I could ever give orders; and the induction physical doctor to answer that I would not follow orders from just anyone who found himself someplace he didn't want to be. I am not proud of it. Indeed, I accept Michael's judgment that it only means some other poor guy without my luck had to go and maybe even to die in my place. I never told Grandfather while he was alive that I'd taken a C.O., although I suspect he knew (and knows now) in the same way that I suspect my father who had enlisted in the Navy and whose brother had been a hero, must have known when one evening at dinner – after I'd already gotten my C.O. – he and my stepmother tactfully suggested that I consider applying for one. I lied a little by saying that I had already applied.

The application was a relation to the context, but the context began to change or be changed, and thus, so did the relation which died and was buried in a place in my heart as silent as Wounded Knee. In the after-decades, because people actually spit on the soldiers coming home – how could you spit on anyone, let alone some poor kid who just feels tired and lucky to be alive, hopeful that he can forget the questions he has seen? – it has at times been publicly shameful to be a draft dodger. There have even been secret times when I almost wish I'd gone, wish I'd at least had some National Guard duty like Dan Quayle. But you know what? Those are the romanticizing wishes of ignorance. Like people wanting to be Indians, these days, to do the drumming without their hearts living through Sand Creek or Wounded Knee or the predawn slaughters of the Nez Perce and the Trail of Tears. Romanticization is a way of not just burying the bodies but cementing the graveyard over, even building a shopping mall upon it, like people want to do in California. No, I don't wish I'd gone, and when I see the Wall with the names of brothers and friends and strangers etched into its black marble, I wish they hadn't gone either. More Coke would have been sold by now if they hadn't.

In the midst of my years of feeling ashamed, of not admitting to anyone that I was what they perceived to be a blood-sucking draft-dodging puny coward, I attended a fiction reading by a tough-guy writer. After his reading, his friend the host writer and he performed their military memories of what a bayonet was for, letting the group around know that they had served and implying that they had served on the front lines. One was a Rhodes Scholar from Oxford, the other highly educated from a very privileged background. Front lines? Neither had seen anything uglier than the black-

and-blue blood of a fountain pen during Vietnam. I was disgusted by their false warrior heroics. I was glad that I could keep what I felt secret where they, having gone, felt obliged to change their desks into helicopters, their typewriters into Bouncing Bettys or Claymores. I thought of Joseph surrendering to the grandparents of these two. I left the reception, went out and purchased a silvery can of whipped cream and took it home where I took off the top and pressed on the white nozzle – aimed straight up – with my thumb until it snapped and the can sprayed me and Grandfather, Uncle and Father, my sisters and brothers-in-law, aunts and Mother and Grandmother, all the ghosts in the room. Bobby could have his politics, I thought, as I surrendered my shame and dug up the pride buried so far down below the loam of questions and possible answers, looked at it, examined it, turned it over in my hands. It was no longer prideful, in its context of change, but it had a permanent sheen, an oxymoronic, shadowed brightness like the questioning doubtful flicker of sunlit clouds fingering the sands and sites of the earth.

X

Politics creep into context, but they creep out almost as fast, and that is one of the dangers of putting too much of them into novels, they can change from Classic to New as fast as Coke and date what you have to say. The only way around this that I see is to keep things personal in a general way, to be self-absorbed (as Elizabeth Cook-Lynn calls it) in an effort to retain your identity in the face of homogenized opinion, and to let questions seep into our certainties. Each novel is a context in itself and the relation of the characters or words or ideas to that context is the lifeblood. In the novel, too much politics is like too many answers, a complete contradiction to the purpose of the genre, which is to ask questions, human questions that the reader can in a general way take personally. Even the best politics need to be a little dirtied by doubt, like the circular, examining essays of Gerald Vizenor, or the questions offered to the general certainties by Carter Revard, Elizabeth Cook-Lynn, or Jim Barnes. Containing their doubt is what causes some people to seem so certain, like Bobby leaving home and country. Live doubts, uncontained and a little out of control, are what allow us to change our minds, to wonder if when Bobby sprayed us all with whipped cream it wasn't just an accident.

Politics for the novelist are like bones. If you leave them buried, you can have a silence that can gather into storm. But dig them up, display them, and they tend to become useless artifacts.

Pride, too, has a shelflife.

All the novelist can do is bury it with the bones and then stand almost helpless at the gate looking in.

9

OF BLOODY PUNCTUATION

Punctuation, like relationships and personal hygiene, is a serious problem in our day and age. It is, after all, punctuation that maintains the relationship among English words the way words do relationships. Even those people who make lots and lots of money seem confused by commas. Semicolons, a sign of education, are used by the crafty to bridge gaps that lie; or they are relegated to writers and speakers who are half of the time assholes. Exclamation marks have become popular! They make dull sentences important! They make dull people speaking dull sentences seem important! They give horns to crows! Now when we learn to speak, we never hear the word "syntax." Minds are filled with freebase fragments of validated thoughts somebody once must have or might have had, and when we don't know how to get any oomph into our sentences (or if we suspect that maybe we're wrong), well, we add extra exclamation marks!!!

Wounded Knee.

Gulf War!!

Big Hole,

Dien Bien Phu!!!

Trail of Tears?

Croatia!!!!

Coyote holds to the hope that the question mark, the gentler twin of the exclamation, has not yet been sent out into the wilderness loaded down with the sins of former thinkers. Partly because the certainty of the "!" requires at least a wink and a nod at the "?". This has happened! demands that we ask if this has happened the way we see it? does it means any-

thing? are we doing the right things? thinking the right thoughts? thoughts at all? pants zipped? blouse buttoned?
. . .

My mother by marriage became parenthetical, always hearing what wasn't said and thinking what couldn't be thought. My father, confused by the effects of the marriage treaty, at first transformed into an ellipsis, a kind of question without implications that would upset my mother. But tired of silences, tired of the rules and regulations that seemed to be imposed on the basis of a treaty he never understood, he became an exclamation. He no longer thinks what needs to be said has been, he makes sure by repetition that it has been said. Tired of laws he has not approved, the same way a reservation Indian may hunt illegally because seasons and points are not for him, Dad goes IN the OUT door, Stays ON the Grass, or sprays toxins on his garden not in a chemical nightmare but in a dream of refusal. Mother is dead, but Dad is a conservative, like Grandfather, not so much from philosophy as from anger at the way the federal government continues to try to control his life. But even there the ellipses that would dodge the regulatory instincts of American government bureaucracy, an ellipsis which allowed Dad to defend a Mexican family's right to live on our block of bungalows or a black man's right to join a business club thirty years ago, an ellipsis, in other words, that allowed sympathy and tolerance: even there the ellipses have turned exclamatory and sympathy become merely the chaff harvested by a combine that eats up everything in its path. When Dad exclaims (Mom is dead), I listen elliptically, aware of my own exclamations that come from my own perplexing inability to understand the world at large or small.
. . .

Why does the meadowlark tip its eye on Dad – and when I

say "Dad" I say somewhat myself since I am like Dad and Granddad in the hard drumbeat of generations – and pour out a suspicion that knows Dad is no hunter but simply a man caught in his refusal dream of technology, wanting to give up all that old stuff and believe in the modern world, in progress, in change for the better?

I remember a scene beside a stream in the mountains east of L.A., Dad and me sharing an army surplus pup tent and cooking over stone-circled fires in pans that seem to fold up like a dream. The ground is moist with the mist of a small but nearby fall and the spongy soak of the drinking earth as we sit on logs as soft as Barcaloungers and hold pans toward the fire that crackles with song, uttering vowels that would make for the start of a melody.[1] The melody is of men, of fathers and sons and fathers of fathers and sons of sons. It took no large effort to reach that campsite, no long hours beneath a pack and frame; maybe an hour's gentle hike, at most, and we brought along enough food to last out the swift and artful dodging of hooks by fish. I cannot even recall the name of that place and can hardly write about it thirty-five years later: I will call it the Place of Good Memory.

I remember another place as well, a hot place farther east of L.A. and south toward the Palm Desert, with white earth bleached in sunlight and granite outcroppings that blinded you with flecks of quartz. My sisters are climbing and scrabbling over rocks as surefooted as lizards; Mother is there, a bandanna tied around her neck, a bandanna that followed mother into nature everywhere because she'd researched its uses as sunshade, tourniquet, soaker of sweat, and signal to planes or helicopters of rescue. The dust is high and our fluids are low and yet Anne or Pat holds up a geode she has discovered, a centering jewel in the plain, black-flecked gray stone of granite. In that permanent instant, this hot place is a place as peaceful in my memory as the dirt lot out behind our stucco bungalow is of a bad, but new, beginning; the lot where I played for hours digging and filling, walking the high steel of dead-branch high-rises or tunneling under rivers flushed full with cans of water and gone as swiftly, sucked up by the dry and needy earth: I will call both places, the Place of Past.

And yet in the first place of the past we are all together and the pasts are mixed in blood and desire, connection and hope; but in the second, I am alone, feeling already a little like Earle Thompson's bottle in "No Deposit":

> Sometimes
> you feel
> like
> a
> bottle
> sitting
> by itself;
> no return,
> just empty;
> ready
> to
> be
> thrown away.   (Niatum, 252)

I am the same age in both places. In the space between inhale and ex-, I feel emptied, as though the Place of Good Memory and the Place of the Past have been hoovered out of me, and I spend my bottle days in that dirt lot, separated by chain-link from the rat-tailed lawn of rough Bermuda which father was beginning to mow sabbatically, hour by hour singing, telling stories that have no endings, dreading the voices of my mother or father even if only to call me in at dusk. It is a happy dreading because in that lot, with dirt beneath my nails and bugs and spiders for my friends, grew the knowledge that was not yet knowledge because it could not be put into storied words that this progress Mom and Dad were achieving was not progress at all.

. . .

Father already felt like an ellipsis, perhaps, and I told myself that after bearing him two girls, when she got pregnant again my mother may well have begun to become an exclaimer, at least in part as a defense against the silences which came from him, doubling and redoubling her exclamations (which had the calm insidious hiss of a snake behind the teeth) as the fetus of the baby grew inside of her. For a while after the baby was born, no doubt because of their mutual feelings of relief – which looked like love – when the baby lived, they got along and in the getting of those early years they did not realize how far apart they were in their ways of describing the world. Mother agreed implicitly not to raise issues as Father's career progressed, the way we children now agree not to raise issues with Father and the same way he does not allow issues to be raised unless he raises them himself, and then it becomes a matter of keeping your head down and waiting for the supply of exclamation marks, built up over those long and lonely elliptical years, to run out. She was a good and competent wife to him by the standards of their day, feeding our five mouths on twenty dollars a week; she was a good mother, too, setting us on her lap and reading to us until we learned to read for ourselves, and although her cooking was awful and we still repeat mother's favorite phrase – "Carbon's good for you," which she believed and which she repeated like a litany as we scraped the black robe of burn from whatever food was before us – she must have managed to nourish us because we all grew into reasonable health. It is true that I supplemented her cooking with dog biscuits, "Fives" brand, sharing the black, charcoal biscuits which were my (carboned) favorite with dogs named Rusty and – a name which measures just how long ago this was – Butchie. Rusty was a cocker with red hair, and Butchie was a mutt like me whom mother stepped on accidentally as she exited the house to hang out the wash and was thereafter as obsequious as any living thing.

Mother, who had good reason to walk around the house with her index finger held up (!) because of her own loneliness and because she already suspects he'll attempt to break his promise that she can go back to school when this last kid is grown (a kid at least one of them must have wanted?), rather than exclaim and make an issue out of it, focuses on erasing the ellipses and turning Father into parentheses. Father helps her perhaps because in part he is helpless to do anything else. If only when she met him at the door, her index finger held up (!) as though she were making a continual point, he had greeted her with his index curled (?) as though asking continual questions. True, they may have resembled two Star Trekkies, for a time, greeting each other with the basic assumptions of their cultures, but perhaps soon enough they'd have begun to feel silly and when one of them held up the index (!) and the other held up the "?", their faces could have softened, her eyebrows raised and his lowered, and eventually they could have smiled at each other. One day, perhaps on the day Anne (or was it Pat?) held up the geode in the rocky place where the wind had blown the water into mist, one of them would speak without feeling the compulsion of previous punctuation and they would have begun again, like

Coyote or Spiderwoman, naming things, inventing verbs to connect them, adverbs to modify the connection, at first in the present tense but gradually, as their language improved, together adding a past and then a past perfect tense out of which would come the need and the concomitant invention of future tenses.

Instead, in that moment between the in- and the exhale, in the space and time of the hyphen's progress, they began to relive a story they'd never heard. "If you'd allow four days to pass between, I would care more for you," Mother said.

Father replied, feeling how unhappy he would be, "If you had me only every fourth day, you'd be very unhappy."

Mother smiled, said it was he who'd be unhappy, her index raised, and Father took up the challenge, insisting that were it thirty days, he'd not be unhappy, and Mother replied that she'd be very contented to be away from him double that, and Father said he'd be content to be away for five months, if that would make her happy, and she replied that the more months the better and so Father rented an apartment up the road believing she would miss him and call him. He moved his clothes out. Mother changed the locks on the house.[2]

It is a measure of the emptiness that the conflict between two cultures can produce that Father must have believed the story he never heard told about how the women grew thin without their men and at long last, having lost their flesh, called the men back to them and were fleshed again. Mother, on the other hand, had long experience with the progress of lovelessness and divorce, and men taking what had been earned by the women – her father's money had all come from women. She grew thin only in her ability to love, but otherwise, once those locks were changed, she flourished and, from a difficult beginning, made much of herself, while

Dad, having lost his stories, added more and more exclamations to his sentences.

. . .

In my own desire for progress, wanting to be in the world and part of it, I gave up my stories and spent a decade trying to finish college. I made myself an empty bottle, a jar placed upon a hill at the center of the world I wanted to be a part of – a center of success, of good grades and praise, of exclamations which were really the result of being filled with questions like Why? Uncomfortable with these hidden questions, I adjusted my point of view with the use of drugs.

A few times, I tried mescaline or acid. One day I took acid alone. It was summer in Davis California, and the student ghetto in which I lived was virtually empty like my bottled self and when things began to go wrong there was no one around to turn to for help, even if I were capable of asking. I laid down. No good. So I got up and walked, concentrating on the image of my feet progressing one by one, left foot right foot down sidewalks and across streets, ignoring cars and bicycles. The sky hated me. The trees whispered at me, each mapled leaf hissing. Thorns of rose and pyrancantha pointed at me sharply. Frankly, I was scared, not frightened in little suicidal ways but scared in a big way that this was what the world really looked like underneath all its cut and cloth. The girlfriend of a friend found me wandering in downtown Davis – her name was Jan and I am still grateful – and took me back to her apartment where, experienced with empty bottleheads, she poured cheap red wine down me by the tumblerful, expecting, as happened, the sensation of being drunk to take over from the sensations of being something I didn't recognize until, after however many tumblers full, I was actually able to sit quietly at the kitchen table and chat with the telephone man who arrived to reconnect Jan's phone.

Grateful, but unconvinced by the imbalance of that one day, a measure of just how much I had bought into the dream of being a part of progress, I kept looking for something to make my point of view match up with the points of view around me and finally found the magic in amphetamines. Now drugs and their imbalances are as boring as Rapid Eye Movements, so I won't go into that decade in detail. I will say that amphetamines became my drug of choice because they made me *care*. They enabled me to pretend "it" was important, and instead of withdrawing into silence they gave me the courage and the energy and the witlessness to speak, much the way I now speak when I am teaching, going on about things the audience doesn't give a damn about, speaking, as we say, from the teeth. They were years in which I learned to understand why a kid from the reservation might take up drinking because drinking makes the empty-bottle need to speak disappear. They were years in which one sister's feelings were hurt because I seemed to turn so much to the other sister, a perception that left me even speed-speechless because the reason was shame, not lack of love. She lived two blocks from me. But I did not want her to see me the way I was, and this was combined with a feeling, whether right or wrong, of unwelcome, a feeling confused by my still-living mother's phone calls and my father's refusal to visit me because I kept living with women without marrying them until punctuation got us and we lived apart. It never dawned on me how empty the bottle had gotten or how much it merited being thrown out (progress hadn't given us the awareness of packaging waste and its technological advancement of "recycling"); the emptier it got, the more I felt as though I belonged among my friends and suppliers and teachers.

Never dawned on me until one night in a chemical haze a story came to me about three midgets or dwarves (I couldn't tell which), prankish little fellows with a twisted attitude who spend their time and energy inventing modern art – the narrator with an editor's indelible red crayon, his black friend Hamm with mimes before a backdrop of performance art such as two subway trains colliding, and when people asked me about "Dwarfheart" in the days to follow and how I'd recorded it all in one night, I meant the answer: I couldn't get the characters to go to bed; there was too much in their world to mess up with graffiti and wrongly switched trains, too many heads to turn, and too many hearts to fill with laughter, and they'd just kept going from one thing to another, all night long.

It was story. Moreover, it was the story of little people resisting a technological nightmare world in which they did not fit. More moreover, I liked Hamm and the narrator and their laughing vision more than any vision I'd had lately and I couldn't help but see that where they were trapped by technology, I had trapped myself, caged myself away from the things that Grandfather and the sister with the hurt feelings had taught me, ruined my stories with systems and success. I began to tend the question marks, even if when someone told me the truth it was only to say "Yeah?" and then retreat in silence. Story and storytelling – as good or bad as it was – returned the power and renewed the character that was my fate. It would take a long time from the writing of "Dwarfheart" for me to be able to walk the sidewalks without any chemicals in my blood and pocket, but eventually the stories would overtake the need to be one with that other world in which I did not fit. That – stories, storytelling and story reading and story hearing and story imagining – and family would become so important that I could not put any of them at risk in chemical nightmares. By now, the family extends, and my heart feels good when Jonathan Corn says, "Give your kids a kiss, huh," and I wonder if my family does not include this Menominee man I know only by voice – on the telephone and through his poems. Certainly, he is a part of my story.

Story taught me to give up drugs and the logical order of wise doubts and in a mixblood dream where my stories mislead perhaps they are culpable but they are never ever useless and they never fail – for lack of story or any other made-up reason. When I gave up punctuation and logical ordering by someone else's rules, I discovered that everything is and it is all connected like dandelions – something Grandfather had told me all along – and thus the story "The Men and Women Who Live Apart" is a story to which in our belief in progress we've forgotten the ending where the men and the women return to each other. It's a story that is not specific to the Sia Indians, at least not if you're willing to see Adam's eating of the Christian Apple as an expression of love even to being exiled from paradise with the Eve who loves him enough to chance losing him in her efforts to get him a little away from old Loud Voice. These stories give us the power to laugh in the face of progress as it busily tries to divide the world with exclamations. Ultimately, they may give us the power to stop complaining and to return to each other and be fleshed again.

10

SO MUCH WATER, UNDERGROUND

As the New Environmentalists, American Indians are often imaged as tree-hugging spiritualists who travel on Indian time, strong but saying few words, willing to be brothers and sisters to any well-meaning person. Some of the more interesting images derive from the sellable package of Wannabe Correctness put out by Native Americans themselves. It is a serious business of anthologies or lectures on the history of the preservation of the status quo. Many of the lectures are useful. But it is also full of trickster laughter to sell nonnatives spirituality the way patent medicine men sold spirits, spirituality which serves as a bandaid for the guilt so many nonnatives relish at the expense of action.

When the laughter fades or when Euramericans stop buying the products of feeling righteously understanding or guiltlessly good and connected — as they must stop if they are to continue being good profiteers because the contradictory pulls of profit and connection would make them disintegrate like a mixblood who denies his mixture — all that remains are a set of forgettables practicing cultural pride on the reservation or in the rundown roadside stands along the Pow-Wow Highway. While Commerce will safely turn an indifferent shoulder as it seeks to catch other dreams, Natives have run a risk: in practicing drumming for their paying friends or teaching them to meditate on the earth-motherness or sky-fatherness of their existences, the trickster-teacher may come to believe the teaching. He may even become the teaching and, in this sad way, begin to look like teacher education majors — formulated lectures, Dead Voices that cannot imagine for themselves a different story, walking exhibits described by anthropologists and ethnologists and saved by missionaries.

Except that we are saved by nothing unless it's the bell, academics do it all the time. Academics, mixblood or not, are perfectly capable of liking what we want to like, imitating it, professing it ad infinitum on and off the reservations. We often finish by believing it, as though there was not a world spinning by outside, as though Coyote hadn't long ago picked up his cubs and moved his den under the cover of cheatgrass and sage brush. It probably begins as a trickster joke: education professors decide they want an expanding market and an expanding market requires more children; they decide that they don't want children to fail, proclaim it as bad, which makes parents and teachers feel guilty, slinking about like abusive adults, and invent an unchallenging touchy-feely emotion-expressing program ("We're all brothers and sisters!") in which no one could fail if they shot themselves in the head because everyone, even the walking dead, has emotions and these emotions are all, of course, "Valid" – as valid as General Miles having Chief Joseph hobbled and rolled in a double blanket under the white flag of peace, as valid as the Native Americans who profess hatred for all nonnatives, or as valid as Coyote when he kills a field mouse or spring lamb.

But Coyote has no emotions when he kills to feed his family, only necessity. Only instinct – that which is a part of his blood and may be taught only to others of like blood. If Coyote took a weekend seminar from some of the so-called Native Americans drumming their way around the country, trying to dance the Deer Dance at Pow-Wows and looking like lame does and bucks, he would begin to feel his Spirituality and his Spirituality would gradually begin to overbalance the see-saw playfulness of his trickster nature. People who want not only to practice cultural pride but also instruct others in those practices become in their likeness missionaries. It is one thing to say, "Come to our Pow-Wow. Enjoy what you may. Buy a craft or two. Perhaps learn to appreciate different ways." It is another to say, "Your ways are bad and of course you want to change them. This is how you convert from Euramerican to Indian. Drum. Chant. Feel. Hug. Confess your nasty white ways and believe these things and you will be saved from the self you have not yet identified and all the saved selves will join hands and save first the lovable trees and then the world. We will drum our way back to the old technologies, give up our laptops and modems, forsake our microwaves, and use pounded tree bark for napkins."

Not only the tools but also the practices can trap one.

. . .

This proselytizing instinct is not a Native instinct. Natives, mixblood or full, know that identity is found in a lonely vision. It may occur in a recognizably Indian way: the vision Tom Joseph has in Louis Owens's *Wolfsong* or the desert vision of Alley Hummingbird in *The Absence of Angels*. Or it may come to you slowly as you, like many mixbloods, construct this strange but beautiful jigsaw of self which is just slightly out of synch with the ways of the majority of people around you, a jigsaw which becomes a picture when you learn that you're a Hopi or Lakota or Chippewa trickster in the cities. "Ahhh," you sigh, "so that's it." "That" explains so much that it is like the keystone to a double arch; now you understand where all those different ways of living and seeing and doing come from. The initial turbulence of this recognition may be slow but more likely it is a joyful turbulence. Like the Hetch Hetchy River crosses California underground only to burst forth in a froth of passionate and happy exuberance which seems violent – harnessed, as it is, by cement in a water temple shrine over its emergence – but is not.

. . .

A mixblood knows, growing up, that somehow he feels excluded even though he has done nothing but try to include. Inviting people to his house, even though it was a house different from most of his friends', he may have wondered why his friends did not invite him to theirs. Or why they invited him only at times everyone was going to be there – like children's birthday parties – but then seemed to forget to invite him when that inner circle of friends got together like rich men for golf or their kept wives for tea after a day spent at "Representing Native Americans."

The hidden story of Alley Hummingbird may not be unlike most or many. In the fifties in Los Angeles, Alley belonged to a group of boys who took up Indian things – held council and pow-wows, made drums and leather articles. The group was open to nonnatives, as long as they took Indian things seriously and not as some feathery joke, so Alley invited his friends to join. Ralph Eastwood did; Bernie Schneider did; Tommy Anderson decided not to keep attending past a meeting or two; and Steve Eastwood was too old. Alley didn't care that his friends were not Indian and if they made small jokes about Kickapoo Joy-Juice, well, he let it go. He was happy that he could include them. Every afternoon when they played Cowboys and Indians, and he voluntarily played the role of Indian, eluding Ralph and Tommy as easily as the Nez Perce eluded Howard and Miles, he looked forward to the next meeting when they would play Indian but he could no longer play but be. He looked forward to it the way he looked forward to the sun setting over the dried-up stony bed of the Los Angeles River. It was a moment when he felt, if not at peace, then not awry.

Ralph, and the more sophisticated big brother, Steve Eastwood, were Alley's friends. But the summer the Eastwoods got an in-ground pool put in behind their still modest house on the other side of the riverbed, Alley began to feel left out. Ralph dropped out of the Indian group. When they played Cowboys and Indians, Tommy and Ralph seemed to be aiming their BB guns not at his legs as agreed but higher up. With Tommy, who could not hit a dead lightbulb standing still at ten paces, it didn't matter; but Ralph had skipped a BB or two off of Alley's shoulders and chest, and his sights got too close to Alley's eyes, so Alley quit. When Alley walked over into Ralph's neighborhood – a long walk, but Alley did not own a bike – he heard behind the high stockade fence the laugh and splash of kids' voices, new voices he did not recognize, different in timbre and tone.

Alley said nothing about the pool, of course. Perhaps he was afraid to find out that his friends were not friends who would include him in everything almost to the depth of instinct. Perhaps he was afraid, given the way other kids laughed in the locker room after gym, that Ralph would invite him for a swim and he'd not only have to ruin a pair of jeans to make cutoffs but also expose his round and hairless body to longer ridicule than the brief showering and rapid toweling at school. Perhaps he was just plain old Native and even as a child too proud to ask Ralph why he was excluded. He was certain Ralph would snort with denial and derision if he did.

One midsummer's day, Ralph phoned and happily invited him to spend the afternoon swimming in his (no longer) new pool. Alley's heart was filled and at the same time he felt ashamed for ever having suspected Ralph of excluding him on purpose. Friends do not question the motives of friends.

"I don't know," Alley said, thinking of his jeans and maybe about his round, hairless body that was all legs and no waist.

"Come on," Ralph said. "It'll be fun." Alley heard some giggles and words in the background. He was happy they were already having fun just inviting him.

"All right."

"Two o'clock," Ralph said. "Don't be late."

Alley hardly noticed the walk over to Ralph's or the change in the world once he'd crossed the riverbed. When he arrived, Tommy and Ralph and Ralph's big brother, Steve, were in their swimming trunks waiting drily for him. He changed in Ralph's bedroom. They watched him change. Tommy punched Ralph on the shoulder. Ralph grinned. Steve said, "Ssssh!" to them. "Hurry up, Al." Alley had been undressing slowly, trying to invent new ways to hide his huge body from view.

He was dismayed and wished he could disappear like a prayer into smoke when they went outside and there was Marily Thompson, the cute redheaded girl who sat behind him at school, sitting in a nylon-webbed chair on the rough stone cement skirting the pool. She wore a demure top and swimming shorts. One knee was raised. She looked completely comfortable and yet prepared and even smiled admiringly at Ralph as he carefully explained how to dive safely into the pool. He interlocked his fingers and squeezed his palms together; his arms pointed at his feet. As you leaned forward, you raised your arms and gave a little jump with your feet to clear the lip of the cement.

"Try it," Ralph said to Alley. "Without going in yet."

Alley did exactly as he was told.

"Elbows tighter together," Ralph said.

Tommy seemed excited. Marily curious. Steve calm.

Alley squeezed his elbows together.

"Tighter," Ralph ordered.

Alley closed his eyes, his tongue stuck out from his mouth, and he concentrated on squeezing.

He opened his eyes when Ralph shouted, "Sec?" Ralph laughed. Alley smiled, uncertain what he was seeing.

"See? He has titties!" Ralph shouted.

"Those aren't titties," the more mature Steve Eastwood said. "They're breasts."

Marily hid her laughter behind a hand. Tommy doubled over and roared. Alley slipped like a frog into the water and for the rest of the afternoon he did not come out until it was time to slink home. Sure that the fault was his, that he must have done something to deserve the joke, he decided to blame pools and since then, he's avoided them, using the excuse that pools are nothing but dead water full of chemical poisons and pee.

   . . .

Such encounters with friendship are not unusual to mixbloods. Able to get along in the European-American world and make Euramerican friends, they often blame the blood itself for some of the confusions and hurts, and every time they feel hurt, the Native in them makes them wonder if they have not hurt the hurter first and thus caused this hurt as a kind of retribution or repayment – something they could accept. Their blood also makes them incapable of telling their hurt directly; at least, the combination of pride, which prevents whining, and humility, which prevents enlarging the pain to the epical proportions of a talk show makes the idea of telling the friend about the hurt at first sort of silly and egotistical and at second unimportant because the friendship returns to normal. It takes a long long time for the mixblood to realize and admit that his notion of friendship is a whole lot different from the notions of friendship that some of his European friends have and that his sense that a friend is like a brother or very nearly a blood relation does not match up with the kind of shallow acquaintance of convenience that so many Euramericans – with, perhaps, the exception of family or blood-oriented people like Mexicans or Jews or Italians – seem to aspire to. Thus, the mixblood loves a friend not exclusively but inclusively, brings his friend into his circle, introduces him to his other friends, wants his friends to love each other as much as he loves them. Thus, the mixblood does not relish having a lot of friends because this depth matters and something less is unsatisfying. Thus, too, when a mixblood recognizes someone as his friend, the depth is immediate.

It takes years and years to learn that with bloodless people this immediate depth and inclusion are mistakes. These are people who would think nothing of seating a mixblood friend at a wedding table of faint acquaintances, thereby implying in the mixblood's way of seeing that he is not a very important friend and the effort to which he has gone to attend the wedding and reception does not matter at all to his best friend the groom. These people would think nothing of not attending the mixblood's wedding or of never thanking the mixblood for the thought and effort that went into his gift. They'd think even less of never giving the mixblood a gift. But in any of these events, there must be blame for the Native side of the mixblood, some flaw or disability that makes him cause his brother to treat him like this. The hurt is repressed, found insignificant given the value the mixblood puts on the friendship. He says nothing.

When that same friend gives a reading from his poetry at the "Y" in New York – ten blocks from the mixblood's apartment – and neither informs his friend nor invites, the mixblood wants not to feel and think what he feels and thinks: this friend is not an includer but an excluder. The reading is cause for celebration, but he excludes his brother mixblood from celebrating for and with. Even then, the mixblood asks himself if perhaps his (best) friend feared that he would interfere clumsily with the sidling acquaintances he can make at his reading? He ducks his laughter at the value of such mutually self-serving acquaintances and instead answers himself, Yes, loudly enough to forget the many nights his friend was too tired to get together – and then he'd find him encircled by more feinting acquaintances at the local bar. The mixblood makes himself see that his friend is right, that he may have met famous people at that reading and tried to turn it to his own advantage or worse (and more likely), said something embarrassingly awkward and out of step. He's not sure he would have; but he might have. He excuses his friend.

But it hurts him. One day he says, "So I hear you gave a reading at the 'Y'?"

"Yeah."

"How'd it go?"

"Real good."

"That's good. Sorry I didn't come. I didn't know about it."

"Yeah, well. . . . "

"If you'd have called."

"Oh. Well, I didn't want to bother you. Make you feel like you had to come."

Uh-huh. I traveled five hundred miles and interrupted the flow of my life at the time to come to your wedding, driving out of my way to give another friend of yours a lift up to where you said three words to me and sat me virtually outside the dining hall so I wouldn't offend all the rich people there and you were afraid that I'd be put out by traveling ten blocks on foot to an equal celebration?

In this case, as much as he loved that friend and as often as he'd admired that friend's work (aware the friend did not really admire his and still living the story that pools are filled with chemical poisons and pee) it is too much and, while the resistance the mixblood has to letting things die will make it take several years, that friendship goes away because the mixblood feels tired and doesn't have the energy to hold on to it. It's gone. Indeed, while the affection remains like a wound, that friendship never was, although like the promise of harvest in fallow ground one seed could change the look of it.

   . . .

Part of all this is caused by the fact that many urban mixbloods grow up detached from the community of people who are like them – other mixbloods in the cities – and I can envision hundreds of other kids and adolescents encountering the same strange acquaintanceships and wondering why anyone would want to call so many people "friends." I can see them wondering what they've done wrong or being embarrassed by what they do feel like Chal in John Joseph Mathews's novel *Sundown*. And now with the acceptance that comes from recognizing the dangers of having my eyes put out, I can see them smiling at the joy of meeting others like them, includers, family people or other mixbloods. It is the gift of exuberance.

Yet from their encounters with the bloodless people, some mixbloods are afraid of this joy. Some people seize upon this exuberance and dam the passion up, keep it contained and tumbling and violently stirred, as though they were a Hetch Hetchy that ended in that temple. They build a shrine to their joy, a temple of Indianness, and they not only worship there, they require others to at least feign worship if they are even to be approached by them. At conferences wearing titles like "Representing Native Americans," you can see the Native American who hates all white people, accepts their money, and then stands before the audience in a pantomime of speechless hatred; at others you hear Indians so bubbly with identity "sharing" what it really feels like to be Indian so that others may "experience" it. Both result from too much head to head with bloodless folks. The former makes some mixbloods worry about speaking out the truth and disagreeing; the latter makes them moan with muddy dreariness or shame.

Euramerican-hating Native Americans standing at a podium may well serve to scratch the guilt that nonnatives in the audience seem to *want* or *need* to feel, but they do not serve Indians. This kind of "sharing" – like swallowing your pride and telling a friend how he's hurt your feelings when he should already know – serves only the guilty, excusing her or him to walk out into the bright yellow light and do the same thing in another or even the same context. Wannabes go to confess their guilt, make others feel or share it so, like Catholics, they're free to sin again. At "Representing Native Americans,"[1] one young German woman rose to confess for twenty minutes her shared guilt in the Holocaust and why, as a filmmaker, she was compelled to represent the historical plight of the "Chews." She ignores Indians and makes Jews artifacts that she exhibits in the museum of her career. A second woman, a psychotherapist, took up another twenty minutes to talk about the Indian in "all of us" and the need to free it from the chains of – you guessed it – guilt. That left only a few minutes for a couple of other quicker public confessions and two minutes for a question or two to go unanswered by wordless hatred. Thus did the exclusion and exclusiveness of the white-hating Native who invited this guilt-response defeat Natives. How could it possibly defeat anyone else?

What exclusiveness does for the mixblood is continue his marginalization, keep him not only out of power but unaccustomed to the odd transformations of power that occur on the conference circuit and in the sponsoring agencies – most often universities. Perhaps the exclusive persona gets money – everyone who wants to feel maximum guilt wants nothing more than to pay someone whose lifeway has calcified around hatred to come and act out that hatred – but hatred, no more than commercial gain, is not the point. Mixbloods have to know this, especially urban mixbloods, or else go around hating a good bit of themselves. The point is to keep a firm grip on traditions or beliefs or ways of living and knowing, perhaps telling about them – but too much explanation leads to lectures and lectures without doubt become dead voices. Speechless hatred, like the white noise of sloppy sentimentalizing, is only a wordless lecture.

. . .

On academic campuses, the reservations created as a way to keep all kinds of potentially troublesome or troubling people out of power, Indians are invited to spend their time playing political prisoner to the bureaucracy that connects them to the world outside by means of money. Money for pow-wows, money for "retention," money for travel, money for monthly lunches of Native American faculty and staff, money for this and that issue. Indeed, the bureaucracy, by doling out small sums that make a provost smile with their smallness, hangs enough carrot before the eyes of Indians to make them begin to think that carrots are enough to live on. In order to get their hands on a bunch of carrots here or there, the university requires each Indian to sit several committees where they can be kept track of – if someone's at a committee meeting, he or she is not home thinking about how he or she seems to be changing into a polyester bureaucrat to which nothing sticks. Even better, the disjointed feeling created by sitting in committee rooms and breathing that fetid air and talking that fulsome talk soon transforms into an active feeling of importance: I am doing something and I'd better get on the horn to Robin over in U.U.D. before I call Tom at the Institute or Bea at Student Services, Oh Boy! Am I Busy and Jeez-Us! there's a meeting Sunday morning at three A.M. that I just have to make because if I don't . . . if I don't. . . .

Nothing will happen.

If I do, though. . . .

It will seem as though lots is happening.

But nothing will change.

I knew a man, once, a "Director of Composition" (a title that was changed eventually to something like "Coordinator of Sharing Self-Images") who, when he did not have a committee meeting he was supposed to attend, sought out open committee meetings and attended them. If you argued with him, his perfection of bureaucratese was so thorough that you found yourself slipping into his way of talking and, if you didn't remember a pressing engagement and flee, his way of thinking. You began to feel a little lost and wandering on Friday afternoons looking not for vision but a committee to join.

Too many carrots, planted in a soil where part of one's self feels betrayed, can make you yellow and sometimes the people who are yellowest create personae which are angriest even until they expect other Indians to be just like them, to agree with just what they agree with. Native American faculty censure other faculty and infected by them, students in the organization of Native American students become exclusive. They make newly arrived Native American students feel questioned, challenged, unwelcome, inadequate as if they assume that the newcomer, the new friend, will fail them. Some excuse this by saying, "Well, they've been here a while and the new student just needs to hang out until he or she is accepted." It does not take long for an Indian student who is made to feel inadequate – whether by other Indians or by art professors who fail to criticize their art from within a traditional context – to say, "I don't need this poison. It's too much hassle," and quit the organization or program as quickly as Yellow Wolf was willing to quit the Lapwai Reservation.

Yellow Wolf was accosted by Christianized Nez Perce when he tried to surrender to "That Indian agent who helped General Howard make trouble" (McWhorter 1940, 278). The Christians turned their backs on Yellow Wolf. These men – like Lawyer, who signed away his lands as well as the lands of the nontreaty Nez Perce, or like James Reuben, who was "in favor" with that cruel Presbyterian, Indian Agent John B. Monteith – refused even to shake Yellow Wolf's hand. Instead, Reuben sneered at him: "You warriors so proud! Too proud to listen! Lots of you killed on the trail. Lots of you rotted on the trail!"

Too proud, one might ask, to listen to what?

As for Agent Monteith's intentions towards Yellow Wolf,

Captain William Falck felt it necessary to rescue him and place him in protective custody. The whites and the Christian Nez Perces were so against him for refusing to give up his ancestral lands and for fleeing to Canada that Yellow Wolf himself would later say of the barren Colville Reservation which the exiled Nez Perce shared with Sinkiuse Indians that it was better there with Chief Moses than at home in Idaho, where the bitter censure of the Christians prevented Chief Joseph and his people ever from returning.

Despite all this, one thing we notice in Yellow Wolf's story is his continuous willingness to assume all men and women are good until they refuse to dismount and talk peacefully with him, until they raise their rifles and take cheap shots at him, until they behave in a censuring, exclusive way like James Reuben or Lawyer. It suggests that for some Natives – proud Nez Perce among them – exclusiveness is not the way. To be exclusive, in addition, a Native needs an agency, government backup, certificates certifying them as "good" and "true" Indians. But "good" and "true" Indians, no matter how many BIA certificates they possess, if they behave exclusively, do not help American Indian affairs. Indeed, they may well be defeating themselves by needing an agency to practice their affairs. Sure, they can practice cultural pride the one or two or three times the governing agency allows them to practice it.

   . . .

The temptations, personally and publicly (and to Coyote, the public may be personal), to exclude the excluders or to mission the missionaries are great. The people who succumb to the temptations are, according to Lee Francis, who runs the Wordcraft Circle of Native American Writers, those who would have you believe that there is one Indian way – which they know, certifiably – one Indian art, or one Indian literature.

But "There is no *genre* of 'Indian literature,'" writes Wendy Rose,

> because we are all different. There is only literature written by people who are Indian and who, therefore, infuse their work with their own lives the same way that you do." Duane Niatum, too, asks if there is an "Indian Aesthetic that is different from the non-Indian." He answers that there is not. "Anyone who claims there is encourages a conventional response from both Indians and non-Indians, and as a result actually inhibits the reader's imagination." Jim Barnes doesn't like terms such as "regional writer," "ethnic writer," or "Native American writer" because all are reductive. "The writer is first a writer, second a Native American, a Black, a Chicano." (Niatum, xviii)
>
> . . .

Out of the break-wall of the Hetch Hetchy's temple, running out just beneath the cover of froth and spray, comes crystal water that tumbles like a Pride of Frogs down the rocky waterway to a lake aptly named Crystal Springs Reservoir. From that reservoir most of the people of the central San Francisco Bay Area drink – Crossblood Indian and Euramerican, Asian- and African-American alike. They turn a tap in their homes and they may be refreshed. No one drinks from the water temple; no one dare lean too far in toward the deafening roar and spit of the water; where one is moved by the unadulterated power of the underground river and carries it like a memory, the river's purpose and nature are lost in its enshrinement.

Labels are bloodless walls to contain power, to ignore what is important and sustaining, like the "temple" built above the Hetch Hetchy's emergence from underground. The exclusions that come from labels — division and classification and certification — are what the bureaucracy desires. It keeps some people stirred with anger; it keeps others, like Alley Hummingbird, insecure and self-doubting; it creates a them and us within Indian groups, as well as without which serves nothing more than greed and self-promotion; it defeats any Indian agenda and it refutes the idea that the agenda varies, and must by its very nature vary; it keeps the waters tumbling up against the concrete barrier and none of it flows out beneath the foam and mist to quench or nourish those who would drink from it — White, Black, Indian or Not — and it never settles into a crystal reflection of what is, a reflection that joins in substance and vision Human Beings to the personal earth as well as the public sky.

Hetch Hetchy is an Indian name.

2. DREAMING

1. Chief Joseph was known to have passed among the lodges of a camp to remind people to maintain order and cleanliness.

2. I describe this scene as reported. However, I want to be clear about my appreciation of my stepmother, who has been exceedingly kind and generous and who over the years has shared great affection with me, my wife, and my two children.

3. It didn't. As experienced as the Nez Perce were with horses and rivers, the crossing of the Snake River in flood with women, children, and horses was accomplished with very little loss of life, human or horse, much to the surprise and tickling displeasure of General Howard.

4. Mark H. Brown, in *The Flight of the Nez Perce* (Lincoln: University of Nebraska Press, 1982), seems to believe that Howard was a just man who did not really want to capture the fleeing Nez Perce. Brown, a military man, assumes that otherwise the Nez Perce would never have escaped the several "traps" Howard and his colleagues set for the Nez Perce bands. But reading Brown gives one the uncomfortable feeling that as objective as Brown might want to be, he is depending too much on the reports of the U.S. soldiers and not at all upon the narrative histories given by Nez Perce who survived the war. Where reports are easily falsified – and were – Nez Perce tellers told their histories in the presence of others who were there with them, a habit which, bringing verifica-

tion and corroboration as well as gentle correction, lends truthfulness to the Nez Perce accounts of Howard's pursuit. In general, these Nez Perce accounts give the lie to many of the Army's written reports. Howard, Sturgis, Miles were all inept, lousy strategists, and the Nez Perce hardly had to work at avoiding them.

5. Old Joseph told his son, "A few years more, and white men will be all around you. They have their eyes on this land. My son, never forget my dying words. This country holds your father's body. Never sell the bones of your father and your mother." Chief Joseph, "An Indian's View of Indian Affairs," *North American Review* 128 (April 1879), 419.

6. For a description of this removal see Fred G. Bond, "Flatboating on the Yellowstone," 1877 (from a manuscript in the New York Public Library).

7. For the photograph of Albert Penn I am grateful both to the Brooklyn Museum Archives (Culin Archival Collection: "Osage Photos") and especially to Ms. Deborah Wythe, museum archivist, for her help.

8. The frame for these revised portraits includes Robert E. Pinkerton's absurd "True Book-Length Feature," "The Indian Who Beat the U.S. Army," *True Magazine* (April 1953) and Robert Penn Warren's offensive book-length poem, *Chief Joseph of the Nez Perce* (New York: Random House, 1982). For the former manuscript, I am grateful to the archivists at the Huntingdon-Free Library, Bronx, New York.

9. Note that "Jacks" are both asses and Indian soldiers in the U.S. Army.

10. An anger that perhaps gave Mary Blue her storied "sharp tongue."

11. A comparable figure, both for his greatness and his eloquence, seems to me to be Martin Luther King Jr. Remember all that stuff "they" used to try to make him less than great? That evoked a response from us, who admired him, to insistently deny his humanness, to mythologize him until he became a holiday as well as the name of boulevards all over the country.

3. UPROOTED IN EEIKISH PAH

1. The list includes Comanche, Chiracahua Apache, Nez Perce, Modoc, Northern Cheyenne, Ponca, Pawnee, Sauk and Fox, Winnebago, Potawatomi, Ottawa, Huron, Seminole, Creek, Choctaw, Chickasaw, Cherokee, Shawnee, and Delaware. For a map that illustrates these removals see Peter Nabokov, *Native American Testimony* (New York: Penguin Books, 1991), 146.

4. PITCHING TENSE

1. Recently, an Indian guest-editor for an anthology of Native American literature suggested to the publisher that I "correct" the structure of the first chapter of this book, "This Close, Coyote," making the chronology *linear*. Color me surprised. I wonder what would happen if the writer had been one of the younger writers included in the anthology who, wanting to be in his or her first major publication, might have actually altered what was a carefully developed nonlinear narrative structure?

2. Louis Owens's *Other Destinies: Understanding the American Indian Novel* (Norman, 1992) and Arnold Krupat's *The Voice in the Margin* (Berkeley: University of California ress, 1989) advance this project with exceptional grace, intelligence, and honesty. Note that many of Krupat's

ideas overlap many of my own, although he presents them from a different perspective and with slightly different intentions. I read this particular book after drafting "Pitching Tense," but the shape of my revisions has been influenced by it.

3. The use of "allegory," here, is a modification of my understanding of Fredric Jameson's statement that a third-world literary author – and there are senses in which this applies to Native American writers –"produces texts that 'are necessarily . . . allegorical'" (in Krupat, 213).

4. The nontreaty Nez Perce (often called "Lower" to distinguish them by one of those ironies of diction from the "Upper" or treaty-signing Nez Perce) never once put their names to any document that gave away their fathers' and mothers' land. If Bear on Top (Wahwahsteestee) signed the 1855 treaty, he was tricked into doing so by the gift of a saddle; and though he is reputed to have signed the 1863 treaty, there is no name on it that resembles any of those on the 1855 document. See Lucullus McWhorter, *Yellow Wolf: His Own Story* (Caldwell ID: Caxton Printers, 1940), 36.

5. SCYLLA

1. Zitkala–Ša or D'Arcy McNickle come to mind as additional examples.

2. In chapter 8, for example, the elder chief La–siah's words are translated into English: "The men will now take women for the final dance. . . . Every man has this privilege. . . . As you circle in this dance, the position of the hand and arm of the man will make known how his heart and mind runs (sic) out to the woman. . . . He must not do crazy things *nor speak the lie with sign-actions. He must*

do the truth towards the woman. . . . All may dance, *but it must not be a mockery. It must be from the heart which should always be true*" (76, my emphasis). As a note on this note, in English, heart and mind should take "run" as their verb: an example of uncorrected grammar; or it may be that in Mourning Dove's storytelling language, "heart and mind" takes "runs" because she does not experience or credit the Cartesian split between the two.

3. See Owens, *Other Destinies*. See also the introduction to *Cogewea* by Dexter Fisher. The case they make for their discomfort, I think, is at least slightly different from the one – or the way – I am making mine. Their conclusion that the novel remains, ultimately, Mourning Dove's is not one I would argue with strenuously; I do think the novel ultimately remains the product of a kind of third person who is a collaborative mixture of McWhorter and Mourning Dove, and it is a mixture that shows its seams and injures the whole. For that, they are each equally responsible, I suppose.

4. This phrasing is taken from George Szanto's novel, *The Underside of Stones* (New York: Harper & Row, 1990), 62. Set in Mexico, I know of few novels that reveal the difference between the native way of life and thought and the "Norte Americano" as well as this one.

5. "Unreliable" refers to the fact that the elders, as Mourning Dove herself notes in her Salishan "Autobiography," did not seem to trust her motives. Elders who distrust a recorder's motives, as many anthropologists and ethnographers should know (and some have realized), often change the stories or omit parts of them, sometimes playing elaborate jokes on the recorder (Sarris's *Keeping Slug Woman Alive* gives a good account of this).

6. THE JACKS OF CHARYBDIS

1. James W. Parins, in his excellent biography of John Rollin Ridge (Lincoln: University of Nebraska Press, 1991) calls these executions "assassinations." I use "execution" to emphasize the tension between the Ridges and Cherokee law.

2. I use the long tale, "My Kinsman, Major Molineaux" as my example rather than *The Scarlet Letter*, which is not a novel but a longer tale with the same narrative and temporal structure as "My Kinsman." The grounding of *The Scarlet Letter* and its dividing point are obvious, one divided from the other in the form of the Customs House preface, whereas in "My Kinsman" it is slightly more subtle, contained as it is in the body of the tale. The argument, however, would be the same with either case.

3. See the preface to "The Fourth Day," with all of its rhetoric and with its sprung tale, a playfulness that is echoed again at the end of *The Decameron* in "The Author's Conclusion."

4. We might note that in all likelihood Twain had already finished *Huckleberry Finn,* and the novel was probably in the process of typesetting. This "chapter" from *Huck Finn* is either one he discarded, edited out, or is an interior oral tale he makes up to give the readers of *Life on the Mississippi* a sense of the way riverboatmen talk and act, as well as to give them simple pleasure in the skill of his digression.

5. While "jacks" may refer to asses, in good voice, it may also include the slang meanings of "posterior" or "Native American soldier." See Eric Partridge, *A Dictionary of Slang and Unconventional Usage,* 6th ed. (New York: Macmillan, 1968).

6. This same claim is made by the blanking out of "Edward ———'s" last name, as if there really is an Edward whose character could be damaged by revealing his true name. These intrusions resemble another example of what I mean by attempts to appropriate the forms of Western storytelling. Not that Ridge read von Kleist – I don't know – but it's the same purpose and claim to factual truth that von Kleist has in titling his novella, "The Marquise of O–."

7. RESPECT FOR WENDY ROSE

1. See Borges's story, "Pierre Menard, Author of the Quixote."

2. Mourning Dove's *Cogewea*, Ridge's *Joaquin Murieta*, King's *Medicine River*, and Momaday's *Ancient Child*, respectively.

9. OF BLOODY PUNCTUATION

1. This is a paraphrase of Ray Youngbear's lines in "Wadasa Nakamoon, Vietnam Memorial": "The knowledge that my grandfathers / were singers as well as composers— / one of whom felt the simple utterance / of a vowel made for the start / of a melody. . . . " (Niatum, 267).

2. Some of this is taken, either verbatim or in slightly modified form, from "Men and Women Living Apart" (Sia), *American Indian Myths and Legends,* selected and edited by Richard Erdoes and Alfonso Ortiz (New York: Random House, Pantheon Books, 1984), 324–25.

10. SO MUCH WATER, UNDERGROUND

1. "Representing Native Americans," The Department of Anthropology, New York University, 2–4 April 1992.

Beal, Merrill. *I Will Fight No More, Forever.* Seattle: University of Washington Press, 1963.

Boccaccio, Giovanni. *The Decameron.* Translated by Charles Singleton. Berkeley: University of California Press, 1982.

Bond, Fred G. "Flatboating on the Yellowstone." New York Public Library Manuscripts, 1877.

Brown, Mark H. *The Flight of the Nez Perce.* Lincoln: University of Nebraska Press, 1982.

Erdoes, Richard, and Alfonso Ortiz, eds. *American Indian Myths and Legends.* New York: Random House, Pantheon Books, 1984.

Gee, Robin, ed. *1992 Novel and Short Story Writer's Market.* Cincinnati: Writer's Digest Books, 1992.

Gidley, M. *With One Sky above Us: Life on an American Indian Reservation at the Turn of the Century.* Seattle: University of Washington Press, 1979.

Hawthorne, Nathaniel. "My Kinsman, Major Molineaux." In *Complete Novels and Selected Tales.* New York: Modern Library, 1937.

————. *The Scarlet Letter.* Garden City, New York: Anchor Books, 1970.

Hogan, Linda. *Mean Spirit.* New York: Ballantine Books, 1990.

Homer. *The Odyssey.* Translated by Robert Fitzgerald. New York: Anchor Books, 1963.

Joseph, Chief. "An Indian's View of Indian Affairs." *North American Review* 128 (April 1879): 419.

King, Thomas. *Medicine River.* New York: Penguin Books, 1991.

Krupat, Arnold. *The Voice in the Margin.* Berkeley: University of California Press, 1989.

Lesley, Craig. *Talking Leaves: Contemporary Native American Short Stories.* New York: Bantam, 1971.

McNickle, D'Arcy. *The Surrounded.* Albuquerque: University of New Mexico Press, 1978.

McWhorter, Lucullus V. *Yellow Wolf: His Own Story.* Caldwell ID: Caxton Printers, 1940.

———. *Hear Me, My Chiefs!* Caldwell ID: Caxton Printers, 1992.

Miller, J. Hillis. "Narrative." In *Critical Terms for Critical Study.* Edited by Thomas McLaughlin and Frank Lentricchia. Chicago: University of Chicago Press, 1990.

Momaday, N. Scott. *The Ancient Child.* New York: Harper-Collins, 1990.

Mourning Dove. *Cogewea, or the Half-Breed.* Lincoln: University of Nebraska Press, 1981.

———. *Coyote Stories.* Lincoln: University of Nebraska Press, 1990.

———. *Mourning Dove: A Salishan Autobiography.* Edited by Jay Miller. Lincoln: University of Nebraska Press, 1990.

Nabokov, Peter. *Native American Testimony.* New York: Penguine Books, 1991.

Niatum, Duane, ed. *Harper's Anthology of 20th Century Native American Poetry.* New York: HarperCollins, 1988.

Owens, Louis. *Other Destinies: Understanding the American Indian Novel.* Norman: University of Oklahoma Press, 1992.

———. *Wolfsong.* Albuquerque: West End Press, 1991.

———. *The Sharpest Sight.* Norman: University of Oklahoma Press, 1992.

Parins, James W. *John Rollin Ridge: His Life and Works.* Lincoln: University of Nebraska Press, 1991.

Partridge, Eric. *A Dictionary of Slang and Unconventional English*. New York: Macmillan, 1967.

Penn, W. S. *The Absence of Angels*. Sag Harbor NY: The Permanent Press, 1994.

Penn Warren, Robert. *Chief Joseph of the Nez Perce*. New York: Random House, 1982.

Pinkerton, Robert E. "The Indian Who Beat the U.S. Army." *True Magazine* (April 1953).

Ridge, John Rollin (Yellow Bird). *The Life and Adventures of Joaquin Murieta, the Celebrated California Bandit*. Norman: University of Oklahoma Press, 1955.

Silko, Leslie. *Ceremony*. New York: Viking, 1977.

———. *The Almanac of the Dead*. New York: Simon & Schuster, 1991.

Swann, Brian, and Arnold Krupat, eds. *I Tell You Now*. Lincoln. University of Nebraska Press, 1989.

Szanto, George. *The Underside of Stones*. New York: Harper & Row, 1990.

Twain, Mark. *Life on the Mississippi*. New York: Bantam, 1990.

Vizenor, Gerald. *Dead Voices*. Norman: University of Oklahoma Press, 1993.

———, ed. *Narrative Chance*. Norman: University of Oklahoma Press, 1993.

Wilson, Elizabeth. *Nez Perce Stories* (audiotape). Wild Sanctuary, recorded 1972.

Winners of the
North American Indian Prose Award

Claiming Breath Diane Glancy

They Called It Prairie Light:
The Story of Chilocco Indian School
K. Tsianina Lomawaima

All My Sins Are Relatives W. S. Penn

Completing the Circle
Virginia Driving Hawk Sneve